I0067337

Negotiation Madness

Negotiation Madness

Peter Nelson

BEP BUSINESS EXPERT PRESS

Negotiation Madness

Copyright © Business Expert Press, LLC, 2018.

All rights reserved. No part of this publication may be reproduced, stored in a retrieval system, or transmitted in any form or by any means—electronic, mechanical, photocopy, recording, or any other except for brief quotations, not to exceed 400 words, without the prior permission of the publisher.

First published in 2018 by
Business Expert Press, LLC
222 East 46th Street, New York, NY 10017
www.businessexpertpress.com

ISBN-13: 978-1-94858-093-9 (paperback)
ISBN-13: 978-1-94858-094-6 (e-book)

Business Expert Press Economics and Public Policy Collection

Collection ISSN: 2163-761X (print)
Collection ISSN: 2163-7628 (electronic)

Cover and interior design by Exeter Premedia Services Private Ltd., Chennai, India

First edition: 2018

10 9 8 7 6 5 4 3 2 1

Printed in the United States of America.

Abstract

Over the years many books have been written about negotiation techniques from many different perspectives. Out of the most famous Western ideologies, the main theme appears to have been to keep bombarding the other side in one way or the other until they say "Yes." Unfortunately, under many cultures that "Yes" can often mean "Perhaps," or even "No." As Einstein suggested, "Insanity is the madness of doing the same thing over and over again expecting a different result." The Middle East and North Korea seemed to be getting nowhere, although one famous negotiation book boasts it was used at Camp David. Then despite all the odds, along comes a Trump who turns these traditional inviolate negotiating rules on their head and breaks years of stalemate. North and South Korea still on a war footing are talking to each other and prisoners have been released. No one has to like Trump the man, but his technique has demonstrated a whole new approach to negotiation outside of traditional norms, which while it might have some unintended consequences, will never see negotiation techniques the same ever again.

Keywords

agreement, anchoring, bargaining, compatible, conditional, conflict, deadlock, debate, distraction, ethnicity, intimidating, intransient, madness, negotiate, negotiation, parallel, ploy, Russian front, sacrifice, stalemate, supplementary, switching, Trump

JEL Classification: A10,13,14,20;B10,15,55;C74,93;D23,47,74,91;F02, 51;H12;M1,16,21.

Contents

Introduction

In 1985 I was signed up by a leading bank to undertake a week's training course under a Harvard program based on the then 1981 famous book by Roger Fisher and William Ury, *Getting to Yes*. Half way through it was suggested that I leave the course after arguing that the work was very American oriented, mainly about bombarding the other side until they capitulated and had to say YES. Having exposure to the Diplomatic Corps from a young age, through my father and then with work for many years in Asia, I knew that often a YES could mean a PERHAPS, a NO, or many things in-between.

Responding to this insult, I went on to write my own version of NEGOTIATING TECHNIQUES and in the ensuing years delivered my presentations to governments and major donors such as the UN, World Bank, EU, and The Asian Development Bank, along with leading bilateral agencies such as AusAID (now DFAT), DFID, Danida, USAID, and JICA. I have presented these seminars in over 50 countries around the globe. Reviewing many other texts on the subject over the years, while they all more or less covered the conventional negotiating techniques, it became obvious that the standard approach might work in simple instances but for major issues they displayed *Negotiating Madness*. Where has the Middle East found a solution and for how long have North Korea's Kims snubbed their nose at the UN? As Einstein is credited with saying, "Insanity is repeatedly doing the same thing and expecting a different result."

Then along comes a Trump who ignores all the traditional negotiation techniques in a digital age and emerges as the most powerful man in the world despite all odds. On the one hand, a contender for the job Hilary is maligned for using a personal mobile phone in an era where most of the 12-year-olds have their own, while Trump tweets how he's running the world on a daily basis with impunity.[1]

In the era of fake news and foreign governments hacking each other's security sites, present-day negotiation has entered a new era. With "Dead

---

[1] Trump reported as using his own private phone suggested so his Chief of Staff would not know who he was talking to, *CNN*, March 25, 2018.

cat on the table" ploys,[2] negotiation is nothing like it has been in the past and, suddenly, whether one likes it or not, throwing the Middle East question open, with America moving its embassy to Jerusalem and agreement to personally meet Kim Jong-un has thrown negotiating techniques wide open. Reviewing the Trump methodology throws a complete new emphasis on what people have followed in the past. He goes along with what the majority of people believe even if he doesn't, and yet sells a completely different message. And gets away with it. This is not intended as either criticism or support for Trump personally but just to highlight his negotiating style.

In the commercial field as an economist, Fellow Chartered Accountant and manager in my own company, I started at military college, have worked for Lang Hancock, the then richest man in Australia, handled "offsets"[3] for the Australian Submarine project with Sweden, acted as resource manager for Weyerhaeuser, the largest timber firm in the world, and participated on various government boards. On the forensic side, I located the secret Swiss [this should be bank as it's not the Swiss Bank] Bank accounts for Australia's then largest tax defaulter Peter Clyne and found the location of the missing Marcos billions for the Philippine government.

In all of life's experience, I have always managed to be engaged on assignments when other approaches have not worked. That background qualifies me in my assertion that there is a need to reevaluate the traditional negotiating skills where old and outdated methods may no longer apply. This new approach, from personal experience, is punctuated with examples from my own engagements working on assignments around the globe. I consider myself an analyst, not allowing emotion or preconceived ideas to influence my judgment. Sometimes, this can lead to what might be considered outrageous assertions, but at least there is always evidence available to back the position. There is no intention to make this sugarcoated.

An essential element of what makes this negotiating text unique is in recognizing that people are same/same/ but different, and this needs to be built into the negotiation equation. What do humans fear most in

---

[2] Raising ridiculous issues to deflect from uncomfortable situations.
[3] Trading off Australian-based input against Swedish.

life if not death? Give them something to address that fear, and they will believe whatever they are told and not question too closely, while at the same time also be prepared to give just about anything.

The presentation here of my techniques follows this inviolate truth, and continues through practice sessions that follow the text, allowing seminar participants to role-play in designated spots in a variety of situations under our new-age philosophy. Some of the roles as in real life are in serious conflict situations with this shown through instructions given participants during role-play. The way the actors perform can also be useful for management to analyze the way people handle the negotiation process. Some people will show flexibility, some will be intransient, all of which might be important for company management to know. Or as I demonstrate, thinking is always outside the box.

There have been many books written on negotiation in its many forms and most follow fairly standard formats.[4] The problem is that while most of the time what these books recommend may be useful,

---

[4] 1. Getting to Yes: Negotiating Agreement Without Giving In, by Roger Fisher and William Ury.

2. Getting to Yes with Yourself: How to Get What You Truly Want, by William Ury.

3. Getting More: How You Can Negotiate To Succeed In Work and Life, by Stuart Diamond.

4. Negotiation Genius: How to Overcome Obstacles and Achieve Brilliant Results at the Bargaining Table and Beyond, by Deepak Malhotra and Max Bazerman.

5. Getting Past No: Negotiating in Difficult Situations, by William Ury.

6. Difficult Conversations: How to Discuss What Matters Most, by Douglas Stone, Bruce Patton, and Sheila Heen.

7. Influence: The Psychology of Persuasion: by Robert Cialdini.

8. Beyond Reason: Using Emotions as You Negotiate, by Roger Fisher and Daniel Shapiro.

9. Winning from Within: A Breakthrough Method for Leading, Living, and Lasting Change, by Erica Ariel Fox.

10. Pitch Anything: An Innovative Method for Presenting, Persuading, and Winning the Deal, by Oren Klaff.

11. Negotiate to Win: by Jim Thomas.

12. The Power of a Positive No—How to say No and still get to Yes: By William Ury.

13. Effective Negotiation: By Leo Hawkins and Michael Hudson.

the world has entered into a technological age where information and its dissemination has become the key to public opinion manipulation. From this the general public can be controlled on a global basis and now negotiation madness prevails. Fake news proliferates beyond anything that has existed before and its instantaneous transmission means that there is little time for human response. This is a whole new ball game in negotiation and can have the outcome of bringing about global changes never before imagined.

Negotiation Madness

The madness started a long time ago. In the beginning. When humans crawled out of the trees or out of the ground and started to look at the sky, they started to wonder where they came from. Where did the sun emerge from at dawn and go to at night? What was the moon? Why did seasons change? A greater question was regarding dying, and what happened after that. Looking for answers, humans looked at the stars, the coming and going of the sun and moon, and tried to make some sense from these events in the answers to their questions. Meanwhile they developed practices to see the dead on their way, from burial to cremation, and even by retaining the corpses or parts of them for worship. In Vietnam, to this day, families dig up relatives two years after they are buried, where the family sits around washing the bones, which are then reburied in a smaller coffin in more sacred ground. You worship your ancestors.

The heavens however were always the driving force as humans thinking the earth was flat, marveled at coming of dawn and dusk and how temperature varied with different phases of the sun and moon. First as hunters and gathers, people looked at how the seasons affected the animals they chased and this became even more important as populations settled and planted crops that depended on regular rains. To encourage these events, humans began rituals to try and encourage consistency with the creation of the first gods to worship, directed at the sun and moon. Wise men came along who tried to make some sense out of these occurrences and they were revered and became cult figures whose words people followed. Obviously clever men, their explanations had to make some sort of sense and it was not long before the tribal leaders were smart enough to engage with the wise men in order to direct the people they had to control.

As societies developed, to maintain rule and some degree of order, it was necessary to introduce the concepts of good and evil. Killing your neighbor was bad, whereas killing a neighboring tribe member raiding your village was good. Again, these local Sharman were employed to set out the broad rules within which communities were to work and, at the same time, to come up with appropriate punishments. These can be harsh as where Australian Aboriginals have an ultimate punishment where the culprits having the bone pointed at them are expelled from the tribe to walk off to die on their own. Human are herd animals and require the support of the herd. Possibly this banishment is worse than having a head chopped off. Rather go along with whatever the herd believes.

With human progression, it was then discovered that an even greater control of the population could be achieved if there was a heaven where you went to if you were collectively good, and a hell for all other activities. To make this thing work, it was necessary to set it into an acceptable framework, preferably with a divine God, or many gods just to be on the safe side, who sat in judgment. In early days, religious leaders found expediency in proclaiming the emperors man-gods as in the local Pharos, which of course scored the priests points with the people in charge. This has continued through history, with rulers providing major concessions (no taxes) against religious confirmation of their divine right to rule.

To keep this whole system working, the clever philosophers who made a living from this thing studied the stars and made predictions as to the seasons and why things happened. They had to be very smart with this, since no one had yet worked out what happened when a person dies. You had to invent things that would appease what could not be explained. It was helpful to interpret the stars and the astrological cycles. Being clever men, they invented supreme beings who could be resurrected for their good deeds and, if not completely returned to earth as mortals, would after death be able to continue an even better life than on earth with a plentiful supply of virgins, even if later translations showed that the word possibly referred to grapes.[5]

Remember that in these early times few people could write or chip stone tablets and only a select few could document these stories, which were mainly transmitted by word of mouth. Overall it was simply a masterstroke to fabricate stories, since now there was a recognized system for

---

[5] First, Virgin at the time really meant "young woman," but all past deities were supposedly born of virgins so misuse of the term crept in. Earlier translations also suggest the use of "virgins in heaven actually meant *grapes*."

keeping whole populations in order, justify wars by having God(s) on your side, and the religious leaders didn't have to prove anything because the outcome was that no one wanted not to have a hope for something like life after death, so were not ready to challenge anything sold to them. Remembering that rulers required armies of men ready to die in battle, so it was convenient to assure these poor souls that they would die for a righteous cause, and a great heaven would be awaiting their sacrifice. Imagine people prepared to throw away their lives if they couldn't be made to believe that would be the end of it.

So how come the world has now 2.2 billion people (in 2010) where 31 percent of the world's population is said to be Christian, with 1.6 billion or 23 percent being Muslims? How can so many people (54 percent alone from just those two religions) accept something that is contradictory right from the start of a Judeo-Christian religion (only 15 million acknowledged Jews.)?[6] With what we know in science today, how can people still believe a God created the world in seven days or the story of Adam and Eve? How do you accept Adam and Eve having two sons, Cain and Able, Cain slaying Able, and then going on to find a wife and start populating the earth? This when, after killing his brother, the only female supposedly on earth would be his mother? It is possible to go on and on over the inaccuracies in the scriptures and the coincidence that ancient Egyptians also had a Horas God, born of a virgin, baptized at 12, preached at 30, was followed by 12 disciples, was betrayed, crucified, and rose again from the dead. Or where before the conclave in Constantinople,[7] Jesus and God had never been considered as one, but this was inserted in the Bible to appease one of the Bishop attendees as the stories were cobbled together into more or less what we have today. Also, not to forget that the white culture backing religion painted Jesus as white, when in reality he would have been darkskinned, never a "Christian," a religion that had yet to be created, and was in fact a Jew. The list goes on and people try and pick issues to justify and reinforce their beliefs ignoring the inconsistencies.

---

[6] Remember early Christians, as was Jesus, were Jews until baptism.

[7] First Council of Nicaea was convened by Constantine I upon the recommendations of a synod led by Hosius of Cordoba in the Eastertide of 325 C.E.

So where does this take us in considering negotiation techniques? It seems fairly important a principle which can get 54 percent of the world's population believing in religions such as either Christianity or Islam, which is in fact based on well-promoted myths. That does not include the other religions such as Hinduism (900m), Buddhism (380m), Chinese traditional (370m), and so on, leaving only about little over 1 billion nonreligious. How do you get so many people to believe something when science itself can prove otherwise? How could they have seen the earth as flat when anyone without instruments can show that standing on the ground, it is not possible to see as far as from up on a tall building, proving the earth's curvature? The relevance of these issues in what is presented here lies in the fact that it is important to negotiate even on complex issues. It is not reasonable to simply ignore an intransient position such as where, say, Hamas[8] will never compromise on the so-called Palestinian question. It must be able to find a negotiated solution to these types of problems and to do so one needs to move from negotiation madness and get back to reality, no matter how uncomfortable that may be. One needs to accept what someone else might believe and cast the negotiations within that context, whether you yourself believe it or not.

Negotiation demonstrates the necessity of pitching what you want within what the other side *needs to believe.* Just as it is demonstrated in religious beliefs, people want/need to believe the stories; when negotiating, you offer the other side what they believe they want and the battle is won.

The truth is that we get back to that first human looking at the heavens and asking what am I here for? It seems a major leap but religion remains "the big sell." It remains the ultimate question and the frustration in looking for an answer opens the way for humans to accept any reasonable sounding explanation so as to be able to relax and get on with their life.

Then again, if you want the basis for negotiation madness, the current most important person on the planet, Donald Trump, in his book *Art of*

---

[8] Hamas's goal is to liberate Palestine including Israel from Israeli occupation with no compromise.

the Deal[9] is quoted as saying, "You tell people lies three times and they believe anything. You tell people what they want to hear, play to their fantasies and then you can close the deal." QED.

Like it or not, welcome to the new world of negotiation.

---

[9] Trump's first book in 1987 was part memoir and part business-advice book with Tony Schwartz.

Nature of Negotiation

Negotiation is in every part of our life. Even when we don't recognize it as such, when you go to a store to buy your groceries you are undertaking a negotiation and completing a contract, you to buy and the shopkeeper to sell under conditions usually laid down by the shop owner. If you go to a retail chain, you may not be able to debate the price you want to pay, but there are loyalty cards that give you something more and receipt slips that can give you discounts on things such as petrol. So even here you do have a slight chance to negotiate. Or you can walk away and go to a different shop.

We start life negotiating with parents; they give us things and let us do things usually in exchange for keeping our rooms clean, finishing home-work, or doing other things they expect of us. As we can also see with over half the world's population following two strict religions emanating from one, one of the concessions children need to make for getting "things" from parents is to receive religious instruction. All of this is negotiation for rewards and benefits, each bringing with it a cost, even if we are not aware that all of this is about negotiation.

Since we all live in communities, there needs to be acceptable ways to interact. In the past before the communications were restricted, local norms were instilled in communities regarding what was right or wrong. Stoning women for adultery can be accepted by some. China executes officials for corruption: in other countries the same people get a few years in jail. Now with global interaction it is difficult to integrate acceptability for everyone, but parents deliver in turn on beliefs they themselves learned as children where they did not really have much choice if they wanted "things" from their parents, and anyway, it is easier to present a packaged religion to a child explaining that when they died they would go and join grandma and grandpa in heaven, rather than telling them that one doesn't know. The problem here is, however, that the children are forced to believe in order to get what they want. Important point. We often have to negotiate within a framework within which we are constrained by circumstances, a typical case being within laws of a particular country.

Later in life we go for a job and here suddenly negotiation rears its head again. Even when applying for a standard position whether at McDonalds or in the Public Service where terms and conditions are set and fairly inflexible, there is still the initial negotiation over whether you get the job or not and, after that, whether you get a promotion away from cooking the fries.

Even in our social life and with emotional relationships, trying to win a mate is definitely all about negotiation, even if no one would ever see it as such. It's what we want and what they want, and the price each is prepared to pay to achieve a specific outcome. Often building up long-term cordial relationships pays off in other ways.

Remember that in trying to foster an ongoing relationship, it is valuable to thank the other side at the end of the negotiations no matter how they went. Hard sometimes after a divorce.

Legal Issues

During the negotiation process and its conclusion, legal considerations are involved. There are some things during negotiation that are not legally allowed and dealt with under the following "Dirty Tricks" and "Corruption" sections. Otherwise during the negotiation process itself, just about anything goes. Remember here that different sects based on religion stipulate that it was OK to lie and cheat people from a different religion, even if not kosher to do it to your own. This becomes important under *multiculturalism* where different communities are supposed to live together under different sets of rules. Offering the other cheek does not work very well when both sides don't believe in it.

To be legally binding under traditional contract law, and in principle globally, in any agreement there needs to be in the first instance the intention to deal toward a binding conclusion, an offer and an acceptance, all of which is basically what negotiation is ultimately all about. Obviously there needs to be legal capacity to settle (not under ages or legally incompetent) and there must be consideration in the deal, although this does not need to be in money.

There are some limiting factors such as the contract cannot be under false pretenses and with lack of consent to what is agreed. In these cases, there are various ways in which the contract can be terminated such as in frustration (if a house no longer exists), but these cases can get complex and usually follow case law.[10]

Within the legal system we have courts having various jurisdictions and different levels. For jurisdictions there is as an example, a criminal side and a civil side. Each has its own rules and can be subdivided under the English system as with magistrates' courts (local courts) for minor offenses under a set amount with no jury, and district or high courts depending of the severity of a crime or the amount involved. All very

---

[10] This is where decisions follow precedents set in earlier decisions at as high as or higher level.

complicated and confusing and a sign of madness when one thinks that an O. J. Simpson in the United States can be judged innocent of murder in a criminal court and then found guilty under a subsequent civil court action. On the other hand, society must have laws to keep everyone in order where there are penalties in fines or incarceration if those laws are not followed.

Other courts of different authority can be for Family Law matters, handling children's (under age) issues, and then as an example in Australia there are Courts of Appeal such as to the Supreme Court from District Courts for cases over a high amount and for serious criminal cases such as for murder and major drug issues.

There is also a Coroner's Court handling inquiries into suspect deaths. At the top end, you have in Australia the Supreme Court under two divisions: the Trial Division and Court of Appeal. Each of these courts has their own rules and regulations, and this can vary by country. Then there are legally appointed commissions and statutory bodies.

Since we are dealing here with negotiation on a global scale, it's not intended to focus on just the Australian system (evolving from the British and in turn from Roman) beyond saying that the law is basically divided into two, statute law being what is laid down as law by Parliament and is meant to be clear-cut, you are caught speeding—you are guilty. On the other side is *precedent,* where a decision is based on a previous decision, which then must be disputed or overruled by a higher court.

Under the British system there is a presumption of innocence. The continental, or French system is based entirely on written civil law laid down by Napoleon as the Napoleonic Code, and assumes that if you are arrested, this would only happen if you had already been shown to be guilty so you then need to prove that you are innocent. The conviction rate in, say, China, South Korea, Japan, and Vietnam would also be extremely high, given that no one is put up for trial until they are basically proven guilty beforehand.

When one then goes back to the start of all this, laws were originally hinged to religious beliefs (back to the where did I come from principle), where you have leaders such as Moses and many more proclaiming that they had definitive proof that God himself had instructed them on the law. Unfortunate that Moses smashed his tablets in a rage over his people worshiping a golden calf while he was convening with God in the wilderness, so everyone had to just take his word for it. However, from this context the Jewish law was developed. Luckily in relation to not killing, stealing other's property and wives, it does not conflict generally with major laws as proscribed in many countries and contains flexibility to comply.

With Sharia or Islamic law, this is slightly different because it applies where the Islamic State recognizes this as the prevailing law, but it is also followed by Muslims in other countries despite a different national law applying. Derived from the religious precepts of the Koran and Hadith, Islamic law can basically fit in with existing country law but would have many aspects deemed illegal in a Western country, such as in approval of child marriage and murder of people perceived to have broken several Islamic laws. Inheritance laws would also conflict in most cases with local laws.

With a separate religious law such as Jewish, *Halakha*, derived from the written and oral Torah, this can usually now be incorporated within the law of the land. However, orthodox Jews also making no distinction between religious and nonreligious life have greater difficulty assimilated alongside other national laws. As with Sharia law, certain areas of Israeli family life are covered by rabbinic courts under *Halakha,* but these when practiced privately outside Israel can usually function within the local laws. Where not, people keep quiet about it.

Otherwise, for our consideration of negotiation practices, the basic legal issues in different countries simply provide a framework within which we need to work, but, in reality, the negotiation techniques we deal with on a global basis remain basically the same. We prepare for the environment in which we are to negotiate by understanding what we need to know, but then do not get bogged down by legalities.

It must be remembered how in what is now a global society, individual beliefs will often vary considerably, but one needs to operate and negotiate within that framework, understanding where the other side are coming from, even if technically they still believe the earth is flat. Yet, while having respect for the other side of a negotiation, it is necessary to understand where the other side is coming from. A Western Christian-based society is at least brought up to believe in honesty, morality, offer the other cheek, and so on, and that is how people are supposed to consider each other. Except that has little effect if the other side was not raised on those principles, or one makes the mistake of believing that just because one was brought up a certain way, the lion would not eat Androcles.

The best deals I have ever concluded we settled between ourselves on a hand shake and then the details were handed over to the lawyers to tidy up.

Ways Negotiations
Take Place

1. Verbal between two or more people, or groups of people

As with the nature of negotiation, the simplest form is between two individuals. In each case the specific person involved from either side of the negotiation come with a *background*. That is our baggage that comes around with us and includes ethnic origin, language(s) we speak, where we grew up, the family relationships, socioeconomic background, education, and, yes, religious beliefs.

An easy way of demonstrating basic techniques is that if the objective of a negotiation is between a man wanting to marry a woman, you need to identify the components effecting the outcome you want to achieve and clear them one at a time, or must negotiate a settlement on each.

Start with ethnicity. If both sides of the developing relationship are of the same ethnic origin, this simplifies the situation and you can tick that off. On the other side, if there is ethnic difference, it becomes a question of whether one party can see whether there are any constraints that might arise and this brings in considerations influenced by either family or friends. As tribal animals, humans want to keep in with their tribe.

Then to ethnicity and you find religious beliefs play a similar and sometimes even more important role in the perceived negotiation. The problem is used to focus on Jewish people or Catholic followers' resistant to someone marrying outside the faith. To do so, disobedience or conversion is required to complete the negotiation. Now the more visible constraints would be seen as between Muslim and non-Muslim and even between different Muslim sects. On the other hand, the Catholic Church is still fairly strong on this issue of interreligious marriage, insisting that children of a mixed-religion couple bring up the children as Catholic. Once more party A in the negotiation must convince party B that the thing will work, some form of compromise needs to be worked out or the negotiation has to be abandoned.

Moving away from the matrimonial to everyday commercial negotiations between two parties, similar situations occur. Party A wants something from party B. In legal terms we have a willing buyer and seller and they negotiate the terms of the agreement. The two parties however operate within a legal platform that defines what constitutes an agreement of *offer* and *acceptance* that can be reinforced in the courts. The constraints can be under contract law or covered by employment law. In our marriage example, it is Family Law. There are also components that need to be present before an agreement can be binding and ways out if what was agreed proves to not be exactly what has been agreed. The same occurs with Family Law if the marriage does not work out. These instances however involve legal issues going beyond the basic negotiation process.

In the situation where we have the negotiations carried out verbally, the main constraint is that if later problems emerge, it becomes more difficult to prove what each side presented to the other so that in other than the simplest of negotiations, it helps to set out the agreements at the conclusion of any negotiation in writing, including sales of property and perhaps even with prenuptial agreements.

2. Written between two or more groups

While most negotiations take place verbally at first, there are times when these can be carried out or followed up in writing. An example, of which many people would be familiar, would be in buying a house. You see the place advertised, go along for an inspection, and discuss the matter with a real estate agent who makes certain representations and you go home and think about it. From there you might contact the agent by e-mail and ask further questions.

Say then the property goes to auction and as a bidder you will be asked to register, and it is certain that on the registration form you will be required to accept that you have had no representations from the agent as to any number of things they could have told you. So, when the property is knocked down to you and you settle to later find there is a public easement running through your backyard, that's your bad luck.

Of course, with property purchase, you get your own solicitor to check out the validity of the title but they may not find that someone was murdered in your new property, making the place far less valuable, or that it floods regularly, making it inhabitable.

So, in the first instance on *Offer* is evoked, which can be a standing offer, such as when something is put forward in an advertisement to which one can or cannot respond. Alternatively, the *Offer* can be requested such as if you ask, "Will you sell me that car?"

The big companies, banks, and insurance companies and those selling shares all advertise but then refer the potential buyer back to reading what is in the "Prospectus or Product Disclaimer," which usually has pages of fine print covering every potential opportunity and loophole since Adam was a boy, and which of course no one has time to read yet alone understand. This is done on purpose, of course, so everyone just agrees and leaves themselves exposed. You want iOS on your Apple iPhone, you agree, or you don't get the system. Take it or leave it. On the phone this is probably fairly safe, but try and argue with your service provider or an insurance company and you will find it is a different thing.

I paid for 21 years on a daughter's AMP policy, so she would have money after university only to be told that it was an accident policy not a life policy although I had the representations from the agent in writing. All attempts to complain said I could only go through the Life Insurance Council whose members were all from the insurance companies. Guess who won? Lesson learned.

Even when going for a job, you will probably be required to sign all sorts of papers or you just don't get the position. They are now micro-chipping employees in some companies. Don't agree and no job. It's like signing on with Apple, sign or you don't get it. (My defense in court would be that they don't expect you to read all their terms anyway; coercion, but that's another story.) The point in this is that when you have the opportunity, check what you are signing at least and it is valid to ask for explanations of terms and conditions if you don't understand or have objections. Don't be confrontational but show your interest. Sometimes clauses are included (by lawyers to earn their fees) to put in everything they can think of. In days gone by when documents had to be typed MANUALLY, only clauses that were necessary were included, but now in our electronic age with "cut and paste," everything is included as a matter of course. In our litigious age, it's also why doctors send you for all these tests in case there are problems, so later they can say they looked. The bottom-line, you can often get clauses removed.

And remember, if you DID discuss a point and question it, should you later finish in court, you can always say that you had queried it and the other side had said ….

On the other side, when conducting negotiations in writing going back and forth, just remember to be careful what you say since there will be a record and, unlike verbal negotiations, it is not much use claiming poor memory later when faced with a written record. Estate agents generally know this and they will phone back in response to a written request. On the other hand, when negotiating a contract by electronic mail and you have a draft contract in your hands, adopt a positive approach such as saying, "I have made a couple of minor alterations in the contract which should be acceptable and attach the signed document attached." This rather than asking whether the changes made are acceptable. Or is sending a contract say, "I attach the discussed contract for your signature," rather than asking if they have any other issues of concern. If they have, they will tell you but don't initiate it. It's a bit like "Marry me" rather than "Will you marry me?"

I bought an Aston Martin DB4 secondhand and was told it had a bit of a vibration in the gear stick over 90 miles per hour. I took it to the agent and asked for it to be fixed. They sent it off to the factory and finally returned it unfixed along with a massive bill. I complained and said it was not fair to be charged for their profit. They said pay or go to court. In court I had my expert mechanic state the vibration remained. The other side argued I should not be driving that fast anyway. The judge ruled that I'd just asked for it to be fixed. It wasn't, so since no "quantum meruit"[11] *had been advanced, case dismissed; no charge.* Lesson: keep words simple.

Remember also that big financial institutions have had their documentation screened by top expert lawyers so that when dealing with these, their documents will always be designed in their favor. Best advice can only be to read everything and before signing, demand written explanations on anything that is not clear or seems suspect. And in reading, don't forget to read the small print since this is where they hide the bad parts presuming no one will take this seriously.

---

[11] Meaning payment for reasonable part for work done.

All of this leads one to the critical part of any negotiation: do your homework! In this, try and find out as much as you can about the product/situation you are to negotiate over, and when it's all over, only then commit the agreement in writing.

Otherwise, yes there are ombudsmen and bodies to whom one can complain later if you have been worked over, but don't hold your breath. Even when there are laws and regulations against certain practices, major organizations including ombudsmen have "Fob off departments," whose only job is to make sure your complaint goes nowhere. So, get it right from the start.

While we talk here of negotiating to win on your terms, remember that if on your way out, such as in a resignation, make sure you negotiate your EXIT. In this, always look to the future and don't burn bridges. Be polite, keep it short and to the point, and remember you might require a reference or expect that a potential new employer will check with a former one from the past. Watch what you post on social media because it can come back to bite you. This is not the time to air complaints. And as with potential and final divorces, be careful of what is being said or posted in anger or frustration, since less-frustrated lawyers can always bounce back on you.

We had a switch girl at one company who was always on the phone chatting with her friends. Resigning to get married, she requested a reference. The boss complied in glowing terms, finishing with "and the best of British luck to anyone game enough to employ her."

So negotiation is:

- One on one;
- One on more than one;
- More than one on one;
- More than one on more than one.

Finalize in writing.

3. Electronically

Negotiating via the Internet has a bit of both sides of the negotiating spectrum going for it. Short IT bites can be laughed off, but other e-mails can be used in evidence. The good part is that when attending to *doing your homework* bit, the Internet becomes a valuable asset. Here it is possible to research the other side you are negotiating or about to negotiate with, look at past history, how others fared dealing with them, who their people are, among others. This becomes a two-way street since the other side can look at you. Remember that what you post online might be there forever and work against you later in life, a warning to young people in particular who may not know what is in front of them. At the same time, consider the validity of some of this information. I keep receiving LinkedIn messages to connect to possible friends even when I know some of these died years ago. And how many people have got into trouble on the Twittersphere posting in a moment of passion?

Some companies are now requiring their staff to contract that they will not go on Facebook or such as LinkedIn so that no one can get too accurate a personal profile that might give away strategic information. This might all be a bit extreme, but such employee knowledge can provide a valuable profile when conducting sensitive and important negotiations. Remember there is now SWARM technology out there, which can make profiles of groups predicting behaviors and even voting patterns, so remember you are being watched.[12]

It should be remembered that a test case in Australia, the Supreme Court in *Conveyor & General Engineering Pty Ltd v Bastec services Ltd* [2014] QSC30 ruled that it cannot be assumed an email has been received simply because it was sent, even if later found in Dropbox. This is important to the offer and acceptance rule in contracting.

Normally a transaction is legally dated from the time an acceptance is posted in the snail mail. This could of course become complicated in events transpired between posting and receipt of the letter. BUT the date of posting was important. Under the 2014 ruling on electronic transmissions, this is especially important since now instead of "The check's in the mail," we have "It might have gone to your Spam folder." The implication appears to be that one must acknowledge receipt for the transmission to be valid. This is important if people sending bills online say you did not

---

[12] Facebook and the use of their data showing this revealed 2018.

pay your account. They would have to prove that you received it. That has yet to be specifically tested in court.

But watch the "Reply to all button." An ex-boss, incensed by an email we all received from a client, meant to reply to us inside the company telling our people to ignore the guy since he was a F… wit. He hit reply and accidently included the client. He then had to try and explain that he did not really mean the client but the salesman in our office. Think how that worked.

As with Twitter, the Internet is great, but sometimes it is good to pause and think for a while before responding since once you hit that send button, it's impossible to take it back. That even if you are President Trump, except with the speed of Twitter, by the time the message is out, the next issue is usually on the table so responses are out of date.

4. Conflict

Dealing with conflict on an everyday level, negotiations can develop into confrontation in business or personal dealings. Conflict can be internal, as with the participants within a family or business, or with individuals, groups, and outsiders. At the extreme end, it would be between countries (or religions Sunni versus Shia, Catholics versus Protestants, etc.). The conflict usually occurs when people have different ideas, beliefs, or theories. Part of negotiating skill is in identifying these differences and getting them working for you. My general solution is to show *Respect*. In other words, I don't have to believe in what you believe in, but I respect you as a person.

Background information helps, such as when you are about to be executed in Northern Africa, call for a glass of water. The local religion decrees that this request cannot be ignored and it sets a different tone. If that does not work, it's also not permitted to kill a mad person…

The small part within the big picture, which most people forget about, is that there is a general assumption that under a given set of circumstances, what we see is what we get. Because a couple is married, we assume what comes with such a relationship when looked at from outside but there can be many different opinions on many different issues which are not apparent. They could even hate each other but must stick around for the sake of security or the children.

A company team could appear to all be pulling in the same direction for the good of the company, but how many people would admit that they really would put the objectives of the company ahead of their own? Why is Joe paid more? Why does Jennie get more days off just because her child is always sick? Internal conflicts exist. To get your deal, you need to first try and recognize where possible conflicts exist on both your own side and on the other. On your side ensure you are not blindsided and on the other team you can use their divisions to your own advantage.

One of my friends had been promised the boss's job after he retired. After working diligently for years building up close business relationships for the company only to be told that someone else was being brought in, she resigned, and the company lost a massive amount of business.

Under extreme conditions on a global basis, armed conflict is a form of negotiation. Unfortunately, at times, countries collectively have not been able to resolve their differences and have taken to declaring war against each other. The main thing to remember here is first that the conflict is usually prompted by one or a small number of people, and second when one side feels picked on by the other. In recent times we have Archduke Ferdinand assassinated as an excuse for World War I, Germany's nose out of joint and Japanese isolation resulting in World War II, while now we have ISIS feeling overwhelmed by the other side of its own religion creating mayhem.

This issue of international negotiation and consequence involves complex moral and ethical questions. Would a negotiation technique to bring about a quicker close to the Second World War have been the assassination of Hitler? Would Mussolini's removal have helped. On the other hand, killing the Japanese emperor seen as almost a God would have incensed the Japanese even further.

Looking at a global negotiating platform, comparing humans to the animals we basically are, we are social herd animals who devise rules so as to be able to live together. Those rules do not always have to make sense, but as with animals, it's what we have grown into. It pays therefore to identify the rules others are working within and recognize these even if logically, they do not always have to make sense. If under Islam, a youngster at 10 started bowing and praying five times a day at, say, 12 minutes devoted to this per session, that would be roughly an hour a day,

365 days a year so that by the time they reach 32, they would have spent almost a full year on their knees. That reinforced belief would be so brutal to challenge, and so personally destroying that it can see why there is prohibition in Islam against questioning anything in that belief. The point being, understand and respect what they believe in and put that aside in the negotiation.

In modern times, we have Russia's interventions in Syria to protect President Bashir al-Assad's regime. He is supposed to be against ISIS on the one side but is under threat of Western-backed rebel forces who are also supposed to be out to defeat ISIS. This seems really to be about those foreign powers involved in the conflict who are gas-exporting countries with interests in two competing pipeline projects seeking to cross Syrian territory to deliver either Qatari or Iranian gas to Europe. Russia wants to control Iranian exports and out of this we have major conflicts. All of this means there is no easy answer but still involves some negotiation techniques on a very serious level. Remember also the invasion of Iraq, which most people believe, was all about oil and not weapons of mass destruction and recognize that there can be many levels in any one negotiation.

Verbal Negotiation Skills

1. Emotion

We all have emotions and display them from time to time. While the general concept in negotiation is that you should never let emotion get in the way of a dealing, this should not let *uncontrolled* emotions get into the equation. Emotions can in fact be a valuable tool to use if controlled in the right way.

As a first-year Duntroon Military Staff College Cadet, in Canberra, senior classmen used to inspect us before bed at night dressed in the most ridiculous outfits. You would be in full uniform at attention outside your room and they would walk past in Jock Strap and tin helmet. If you laughed, they would demand, "Wipe it" and you'd have to wipe the smile off your face with your hand. You'd be sent back to dress properly and parade again where now you were as they had been and them in full uniform. Again, you were not permitted to laugh. Their argument was that if we paraded before the Queen and her hat blew off, we could control ourselves so as not to laugh. The bottom-line was that we became very good at controlling emotions. The only times anyone has since ever seen me angry was in a controlled reaction.

Other negotiation books talk about not bargaining about positions and separating the people from the problem. This assumes you are in a position to dictate how negotiations are to take place. Tell that to a Trump. OK, Apple might be able to dictate to its customers on whether to take their phone as they designed them, but there is still competition with other companies and a fair bet that negotiations on design go on at length within Apple itself.

Demonstrating excitement and enthusiasm can drag the other side along with you, when you show how great working together will be and outline all the benefits this would bring. Get in with a group of fun people, and it's easier to carry people with you as long as you don't lose the objective.

Displaying negative emotions and a grumpy face can also have an effect. You might want to show that something you quite want is not that great so as not to encourage them to ask for something else.

Emotion can also affect your own performance. It has been shown that when faced with a water hazard, a golfer who stands there and thinks, "I'm likely to hit the ball into the water," they most often will. Those who believe they will clear the water generally do. Glass half full. Back to the God concept and it's all about self-induced faith. God will help me do it. Different from *the Little Steam Engine's* "*I think I can.*" Of course, if God does not come through, the thought might be that he was just too busy and better luck next time.

Anger as an emotion is only to be used in exceptional cases as it can derail a whole negotiation if not used correctly. When applied at all, it should be hinged on something appropriate to invoking anger. Say for example someone has made a gender or race inappropriate comment, displayed anger could set the other side back and prepared to make concessions they would not have considered otherwise.

Remember to look for emotional stress on the other side. Perhaps they have been given instructions such as, "Don't come back without a deal," which could be stressful for them. In that case, you might be able to give them some concessions and help them out in exchange for something on your side. This could be as with offering a cheaper model, lessening warranty, and so on. There is usually not just one answer to a problem.

Running a large pastoral company dealing with farmers, we found a main selling item was electric drills, where we ordered 3,000 at a time. Instead of buying from an importer I went to Taiwan where our main model came from and asked the supplier, "How much?"

The Taiwanese said, "How much do you want to pay?"

This seemed like a stupid question to me, but they explained that they could let us have a $50 drill or a $100 drill, the difference being that the cheaper drill would only last half the time. There is always a way out.

There was this old guy trying to park his Jaguar but as he reversed back a young guy zipped in and took the space. Getting out of his car he said to the old guy, "How would you like to be young enough to be able to do that?" The old guy put the Jag into gear and rammed the young guy's car saying, "And how would you like to be old and rich enough to do that?"

Perhaps not a politically correct story but it makes a point.

Then never forget the religious connotation. You might be dealing with people where you cannot understand their beliefs, but they may be important to them. Don't get frustrated.

Bottom-line mantra with emotions, "Don't get mad, get even."

2. Handling of language

There are a number of sides to the language question.

If negotiating with the other side in both your native languages, it helps to adjust to the same level. Don't "highbrow" to people who don't converse on that level and in Australia, for example, if you deal on a *mate ship plane*, this is like speaking to someone on their own level and can be helpful achieving the desired ends.

When dealing with other language speakers, consider both language and culture. On the culture side, things such as touching people on the head, pointing toes at people, handing things to people with the left hand, or going to shake women's hands, let alone kissing them on the cheek, are some of the cultural no-noes to avoid.

On the language side, while it is unlikely that people unfamiliar with a language will utter words offensive in another language, there are words that mean different things in different languages, hence there is a need to understand the differences.

Americans are generally very forthright and can tell you their life's story on a first meeting, while other cultures are more reserved. Asians generally protect their privacy and usually only offer personal details in response to a specific question and, even then, they will usually offer the answer they expect is required. While Westerners are happy to offer details of spouse and children, Asians almost never volunteer such family information unless it is requested, and the sense is always that this is offered reluctantly. The point is that building familiarity reduces the likelihood of being cheated. Perhaps they understand that this provides information that could be used to get closer to them and compromise their negotiating position.

A common mistake foreigners make in many countries is to try to impress by learning and then speaking the local language. While this could be considered a compliment to the host country, experience shows that it does not work. A good example of this going wrong would be in the case of former Australian prime minister, Kevin Rudd, who prided himself on his Mandarin. This is usually considered condescending and very "Uncle Tomish." That does not mean that it's not worthwhile learning local languages and worthwhile when you know what others are saying believing you don't. But don't push it.

Negotiating a multimillion dollar timber export deal with the Japanese, they kept switching to Japanese between themselves, which was annoying. At one stage I interjected with "Sorry I did not say that" to which they responded, "Oh you speak Japanese?" Obviously, I didn't but they could not be sure so never switched to Japanese again and had to keep things out in the open.

The Americans tend to accept that everyone will deal fairly evenly and most things will be up front. That does not mean that they will not use ploys or even dirty tricks, but generally they believe that they are right, their products are good, and people should accept them at face value. A YES is usually accepted as a YES and a NO a NO.

In most of Asia, it is considered impolite to say "NO," so a No will usually be presented as a "Yes" but in many different forms from "Perhaps," to a final but unlikely straight out "No." In many cultures, it's all about FACE. It's not just what is done but how it's done. In China, a common precept is, "As soon as the contract is signed, the negotiations begin."

In Hong Kong, I went to a big lunch of a Chinese colleague launching his new book, only to get a bill for my share of the lunch after the event. September 2015 and an Australian front bench Senator, Labor's Sam Dastyari, had to step down because he had one of his Chinese contacts pay a bill. Australians didn't understand this, but the Chinese would be wondering, "What's the big deal."

This raises the question of presents. In China, giving and being given presents is a normal thing and almost a requirement. One thing they seem to like for some unknown reason is giving framed pictures of cats. Most of the presents can be of no great value but are seen as part of a bond. The same goes for the banquets where in China these had to have at least 20 courses, and no business is discussed before serving of the fish dish coming around half way through. The guest sits furthest from the door where whoever is paying the bill sits. The host pays but in typical

Chinese tradition which Dastyari's detractors did not understand, you might finish paying anyway.

Handing out donor money in China, we would run seminars and training sessions around the country and, in doing so, pay various hotels for venue rental and accompanying food. The Chinese side handled those negotiations where I learned this included banquets they hosted in our honor, but we were paying.

The lesson is to watch and learn local customs and ways of doing things, trying to fit in and temper different cultural practices.

Contracting in China, a common occurrence from my experience was that in response to a tender, top-level equipment would be specified from European companies along with glossy brochures and technical specifications from which someone would win the tender. In execution, however, it would suddenly emerge that the European model would have been replaced by a locally manufactured unit, which would be a copy and of course at a lesser price to the contractor. When challenged, the argument would be that the quality is the same, but it is just cheaper. The counter offer would be that we go ahead, but having been caught, we split the savings. Of course, they had won the contract on the superior European quality and might not have won on local specifications thereby creating a dilemma. This is particularly so if construction was well under way. If won on a donor contract, there are rules that prevent this going ahead but even then, these agencies want to minimize costs and just have to go ahead but then try to be more careful next time.

Comments on cultural positions can also create problems if you don't understand. One issue is about food served: how do you react if served dog, or in Korea still wriggling octopus tentacles on your plate? You have to work that one out for yourself depending on how important your negotiations are, and how much or little you worry about offense.

Watch also what you say.

Alex Gordovich on his first mission with me to Korea, driving through town, asked our host if all the big earthenware pots on the baloneys we passed were for night soil? This was of course a major insult to the family's store of homemade kimchi.

Later he freaked out at dinner when the front end of the live crayfish on the table walked away from the back end.

3. Speed of conversation

As with control of emotions, the speed of delivery in a negotiation can have a significant outcome on the result. First up, rapid enthusiasm helps a deal along, while monotone delivery can put everyone to sleep or wanting to bow out and go home. Conversely, too much enthusiasm can put the other side off or make them think there must be something wrong. Usually there is an intermediate position.

Speed of discussion is also important when dealing with people where a different language is involved. Ensure that the other side understands what you are saying, or you can be wasting your time. When you have a team, try and pick the best speaker to get the job done for you.

I was called into the finance director's office one day to meet he said the best rural accountant in the country. We discussed some of his client's accounts and I watched this accountant drift from one subject to the next, backtrack, and at times seem to lose the plot all together. After he left and I sat there shaking my head, the director said, "Good isn't he?" I didn't understand until he explained that with this guy representing you at the tax office, no one could follow him and he got away with anything just by this act.

4. Ethnicity

Dealing with different ethnic groups brings with it the need to apply appropriate negotiating techniques. In Japanese negotiations, the man leading the negotiations might not be the person in the group calling the shots. He can be the little guy sitting up the back seemingly half asleep but nothing will move ahead unless he is happy. Something to watch out for.

In one group of negotiations, the Japanese brought this team and an old man at the back regularly fell asleep. It turned out however that he had the final decision, which had already been made, so we went through four days of negotiations to save face while he enjoyed his holiday.

Having dealings with government trade ministries, they used to send me team after team of Japanese visitors supposedly out looking for business opportunities. I spent hours giving them the talk while they took copious notes. Nothing ever came back from these teams until I learned that they were just on company paid holidays but didn't know what else to do with their time but take notes and submit reports on their return home.

In Indonesia, China, or elsewhere as a general rule, it might be a good idea to establish whether the people present are able to undertake the negotiations and capable of concluding an agreement. Otherwise, days of discussions can take place without any resolution and after being worn down another group takes over. A similar issue found with the Japanese is the continual rotation of people in a negotiation. If that behavior starts, it is good to say that if their side is tired, we adjourn to let everyone have a brief rest. They will get the message. Without this, you are playing into their hands and giving in to their insult.

Be careful in presentation. In Indonesia, we had a noted Kenyan agriculturalist related to the famous Professor Leaky leading the presentation to the general in charge of the research establishment. Leaky told him that he had taught many Africans and so Indonesians should be able to grasp the essentials. This did not go over very well with the general and we were told to keep our man out of the way. This one incidence plagued the rest of the negotiations.

Alcohol also plays an important part in Asian negotiation. This has many dimensions and can vary greatly with the level of people you are dealing with. In China as an example with its ritual drinking, downing drink after drink of rice wine, part of this can be celebration while another part is to see how much the foreigner can drink, and whether he (or on limited occasions, she) will continue until he makes a fool of himself. The main thing to realize is that this is not simply social but becomes part of the negotiation process. Refuse to take part and it's held against you, make a fool of yourself, likewise. Drink but hold on until you declare enough, and it is held in high esteem.

If you find you are being sandbagged by teams of people trying to "Gumbay" you so that you finish on your ear, it is still polite and also considered appropriate to decline and, for example, elect to drink with just one person.

After delivering a lecture at a University in China, all of the students lined up wanting to drink a toast with me. They might have been wanting to get back at me for the lecture, but I was not having any of it. I said point-blank that I would drink as much as they liked with anyone they nominated as their representative but couldn't be expected to handle everyone. This was respected rather than having to make a fool of myself and losing respect.

In a Japanese context, when I was an important customer hosted at their favorite Melbourne Japanese restaurant, I was seated at the head of the table with 10 executives and the Japanese Australian manager. I was plied with toast after toast of Chivas Regal 12-year-old Scotch from what they called the "Client bottle," while the other 10 were drinking from Johnny Walker, "Staff bottle." After a few drinks, I noticed that I was getting light headed while there was no effect on the Japanese. I said that since we now knew each other so well, I would drink from the "Staff bottle" and they should have the "Client bottle," where upon I poured their drinks to find that they had all been drinking tea. Not able to lose face, none of the Japanese admitted to the deception and had to drink Chivas for the rest of the night until their manager was carried comatose from the room. Another time I had to eat "Fugu" or puffer fish while the other Japanese dinner guests looked on as if to see whether I would survive. Some of the things one needs to do to be taken seriously in negotiations.

In Korean drinking sessions, these can become like Russian roulette. Everyone around the table has a glass of beer. Someone finishes their glass and it's not done to leave an empty glass, so someone drains theirs and filling it, offers the full glass to the person who finished first. But that leaves them with an empty glass, so someone else quickly follows suit. Deadly system as there really is no end. Remember also, in Korea, wearing sunglasses is a No No. It's considered disrespectful as if you are trying to hide your eyes so people cannot look into them and you have something to hide. In other countries, sunglasses are used to intimidate.

In Poland, Albania, and other parts of Eastern Europe, it can be hard liquor at 10 a.m. until it is possible to forget what the negotiation was all about.

Dealing with Americans and alcohol can also have its problems.

Entertaining a senior American on his first visit to Australia, I took him to one of my favorite restaurants for dinner. We had a few predinner drinks and then went on with a white wine for entre of fish and then a Merlot Red with the steak. We finished with a Brandy and coffee where upon my guest was not feeling too well and needed to go to bed. Later he explained that in the States they got stuck into the predinner drinks but did not have alcohol during the meal. He had loaded up early in this belief.

Do your homework before ethnic involvement.

1. Phase One: Preparation

(i) Homework

The need to do your homework before entering into a negotiation you are serious about cannot be stressed enough. Following on from the previous section, as an example, in Vietnam, there are different forms of address for people older, younger, or senior. People often think it is rude when straight off Vietnamese will enquire about your age when they are just trying to find out how to address you.

On homework, starting from the position of a sales person, the preparation has to be an intimate knowledge of your product and what it is competing against by other compatible or nearby offers and your competitors.

If you are the buyer, a similar situation applies. You need to know about features, warranty, and price; the history of the store (Dick Smith in Australia didn't help when it went bankrupt after floating despite the founder's name); and the background of the people you are dealing with. Obviously, the amount of research you do will depend on the importance of the deal you wish to strike; but if one starts doing homework on simple issues, the mentality will follow you into the big ones. Homework then follows into specific areas.

(ii) What do you want?

Remembering the part about doing your homework, the first question as if you are formulating a business plan is to determine exactly what you want out of a negotiation, whether personal or commercial. Are you buying or selling?

For example, you are a salesperson for the XTRA Computer company who wants to sell one of your latest wiz bang super computers to a Russian company that wants to upgrade its internal statistical capability. You want to make one sale of $3.5 million covering cost, insurance, and freight (CIF), delivery within three months on site in Russia with a six-month service contract and warranty, after which they are on their own with no further warranty. Throw in that their technicians can come to your HO at their expense to study the full potential of their new system.

Offer a price reduction to $3m for a subsequent computer if they require.

Offer a new operation system at $500,000 to connect their computers to the new system.

The options for outcomes are as follows:

WIN–WIN: Both sides get what they want.

WIN–LOSE: You win but they lose.

LOSE–WIN: You lose but they win.

LOSE–LOSE: Both sides lose.

But make a plan along the line of what can be called a Road Map. Onto the plan you can plot in deviations so that your real final goal is not obvious, can throw in red herrings and offer proposals you don't really want accepted. You never deal with the whole hand up front. You can even imply that you can walk away.

Webster & Woolgrowers Ltd. had the Fiat tractor franchise for Tasmania. We were sent a memo from Sydney head office that we were not selling enough tractors and we should front and be put on the carpet. Director Jim and I flew to Sydney and headed out to Ryde. After being chastised, which we did not appreciate, Jim upped and we walked off down the street with the Italian Fiat managing director following us to apologize. The meeting resumed where we explained that their tractors were not suitable for the hilly country in Tasmania and we were lucky we sold as many of their tractors as we did. We got our apology, an increase in margin, and a sizable advertising budget, all from just walking away.

And as with any good Plan A, always have a Plan B, Plan C, and so on, just in case.

You are going into a negotiation where ideally you want both sides to win. You do not want both sides to walk away and lose. Ideally, if not a Win–Win you want to be on the winning side, so you plan accordingly.

Whatever you do, do not go into a negotiation before you know exactly what you want to achieve.

> Have Plan A—Ideal achievement
> Plan B—Fallback position
> Plan C—Retreat position
> *MINIMUM ACCEPTABILITY*
> *MAXIMUM ACCEPTABILITY*

(iii) What do you think they want?

Entering the negotiation, you might expect that they will want a lower price and an extended warranty.

When looking at what the other side might want, don't just stick to the obvious. Look at what you might want if you were on the other side and think outside the box, so you don't get blindsided. For example, they might be a big company but still demand time payment or other warranties. Trump dealing with North Korea understands the power of ego. He understands the one thing Kim wants more than anything is not nuclear weapons, not world domination, or the well-being of his people, BUT he wants to be recognized as a player at the BIG table with the BIG boys. Trump gives it to him and suddenly there are talks between North and South, which has not happened since the end of fighting between North and South.

Remember that perceptions play an important role. It is not always what is the reality of a situation but can also be what people perceive it to be. This means both sides should ensure they are talking about the same thing. Determine also what is their need. Their perception might be different from yours. Or they may have an unfulfilled need that no one has thought about.

In the example of the 1975, upcoming Lake Gordon flooding for the hydro scheme in Tasmania, there was concern that the flooded forest timber would be wasted. Every Australian timber company tried to find a solution where they could use this timber with no result. I found a Japanese company Marubeni, who had a Japanese client having just completed building a chip mill to be sourced from Brazilian trees. Brazil, I learned, would not be ready to ship for two years during which time the Japanese plant would stand idle.

We could fill the gap. With this proposal put to them, the Japanese came to the party, and with government approval, eight full shiploads of logs were sold for the highest price for timber ever achieved from Australia. Thinking outside the box.

But watch perception.

In another instance I went with a rugby team to play the Seychelles. We were met at the airport by our counterparts and entertained lavishly that night. The only problem was that those were not the team we had to play but their Second Team we thought would be easy to beat, but it was only when we got to the actual match we met their Number One Team, with us all slightly the worst for ware. Totally blindsided.

Remember also that people usually look to their own interests, even if they have to tailor these to fit within the group.

(iv) What is their history?

Doing your homework, you know that this company is a leader in their industry and are used to getting their own way.

In early jobs with the Food and Agricultural Organization of the United Nations, I was always worried that when I negotiated the next contract my financial demands would exclude me from consideration. It took about two years before I learned that recruitment was a two-stage process, the technical people chose you and then told the HR people to finish the recruitment at any reasonable price. So HR offers you a P5 when you already had that and want to move ahead to D1. Not good if you could be beaten down in salary or to P5 not knowing that.

The history of the company is important along with the history of the individuals in their organization. Sometimes the situation itself can be part of history and you can lay down warnings ahead of time.

In my first assignment in East Africa, the Tanzanians had just driven Idi Amin out of Uganda and returned home the heroes, notwithstanding that they had shot down President Nyerere's son by accident when his fighter overshot Bukoba onto Lake Victoria and returned with his plane mistaken as one from the enemy. Nyerere told them to go back to plowing fields. They said NO, we are heroes and gangs of armed men raided houses every night. With my team of five, four of them were robbed at gunpoint in their homes. Two of the wives were raped. The police said we can't help you but if you want a gun we'll give you a license.

So, when there was noise outside at night I'd be out in the garden, licensed gun in hand, with a towel wrapped around me and the night watchmen "askaris" hiding in the bushes. Of course, the askaris drank at the same pub as the robbers the next day and would rave about how their boss was mad, had a gun, and wanted to kill someone. The robbers would ask for our address and we were marked to be left alone.

(v) What is the history between two sides?

If there is no real history of commercial dealings between the two sides in the past, have one of their technicians been to visit and is there any known contact? Obviously, it is helpful if there is some history between the two companies and whether there was successful negotiation, when and by whom.

(vi) What do you want as an outcome?

This is where you decide what you want, but what is the lowest point you might like to aim for, what is the lowest price, and what things you can sacrifice in order to get the sale? In a political setting, few people get their full legislation passed without interested parties having amendments for issues they find important. The main thing is not to lose sight of the overall objective.

In the same political context, the elephant in the room is always whether the legislation is the most important to the individual or the chance for reelection. When working on party platforms, there is the toss up between toeing the party line as against doing what you believe in and risking the ire of the party. Then again along comes a Trump, takes on his own party to win a nomination, and then a presidency.

(vii) What are the negotiable issues?

Almost anything, most of the time, is negotiable. Intransient positions are covered later.

On your part, when you are making a plan you can outline what you want to negotiate. Perhaps you want to focus on a "bottom-line" but not on warranty, as that could get expensive. Just be careful that when you preset a bottom-line you don't lock yourself in. If a unit you are selling is to be a suspended line, any price could be better than nothing.

Negotiable issues refer to what can be discussed to take the focus of the central issue on, first, in this case, getting a sale at any price but preferably at the full asking price.

Remember you are trying to obtain the best possible deal.

(viii) Is there a hook?

A hook can be something designed to get their interest. In simple forms, it can be handing out football jerseys for a favorite team, or free samples of the product you are trying to sell. Bottles of good wine have been used as inducements. This is not really bribery if the value of the items is small but gets complicated where say an old bottle of Penfold's Grange Hermitage can cost a few thousand dollars. One NSW Premier lost his job for not declaring such a "gift."

Currently, with online marketing, it is very common that people send out what they believe are interesting stories into your mail box or phone where upon you are then inundated with solicitations to buy any number of products they are selling with multilevel marketing, or from people trying to sell you a better website even when they don't manage to write in English.

A hook can also be on a personal footing where you or one of your team is a friend of someone on the other side, although this could work against you. In Australian politics, the head of a party could have an in-law as Governor General.

(ix) What are issues in order of importance?

The price is the most important. The other side must also NOT know that there is a new advanced model hitting the market in 12 months, which would make the current one obsolete. Yet remember you need a comeback if they catch you out and say, "Why did you not tell us?"

When ranking importance, it is essential not to forget that personal issues need to be taken into account. For example, will the negotiator lose their job if the sale does not go through? Will they be promoted on success?

(x) What are possible "throw-aways?"

In negotiating, it is useful to build in throw-away items you might look like wanting but would sacrifice to close the deal. An example would be backing down from Business Class travel to Economy class rather than accepting a lower fee for a job.

These items or issues are peripheral but can work in your favor.

During the 1970s mining boom in Australia when everyone was scrambling for geologists, my friend who was in hot demand had many contracts offered him and had to negotiate the price. In each case, he was prepared to lower his fee rate but insisted on 10-year contracts. When the mining boom came to an end, he was laughing, since no matter how little his retainer, he was still being paid out to 10 years.

Always build into offers things that could look good but that you can sacrifice during negotiations rather than having to make unwanted concessions.

(xi) Are there supplementary offers?

For example, when the second computer offer is a red herring since that line will be discontinued.

Where research pays off, there might be something the buyer could want that the company could also sell as an add-on in either material or service. "Do you want fry's with that?"

(xii) Redefine "bottom-line."

At some stage of the negotiation plan, it can be necessary to decide you are not going to win and instead be flexible, such as when you "need to get rid of this computer at any cost but not to let their side know this will soon be outdated."

When you have completed your plan, it is a good idea to put this down on paper and keep it in front of you even if it is just in bullet points. In the heat of the moment it can be distracting and a person can go off target. If the plan is in front of you, it is always possible to go back and recover. Remember the other side can be trying to put you off your game, which is possible if a curve ball comes in which you didn't plan for, such as if they suddenly announce that they know your computer will soon be outdated.

Make sure that you keep the paper plan a secret.

One major Japanese Trading House used to negotiate this big timber deal with me in Tokyo. Come lunch time and as we went out they said for that I should leave my briefcase as it would be perfectly safe. After lunch I noticed that while we were away someone had been through my case and presumable had copied my game plan. After that I used to leave "red herrings" in my case for them to find. It helped a lot on price. Now I have a briefcase with a combination lock.

Research, Research, Research...

Do your due diligence, the other side's strengths and weaknesses in a SWOT analysis, just as you do your own. Organizations have agendas as do individuals.

(xiii) Going off the rails

During negotiations make sure that the FEELING is right. If something does not have a good feeling about it, try and defer the discussion or at least have a break while trying to identify what is wrong. This might be prompted by something someone might say, which throws in a curve ball, or it could be certain interchanges between parties on either side or with the other side.

In a certain court case of mine, I was doing quite well with charts and calculations but could not understand why the other side and the Judge were smiling at each other. After losing the case I learned the street I was talking about had been moved and all of my calculations were of no use.

In Japan my Australian team could not understand how the Japanese had inside knowledge of our discussions only to find a microphone in the hotel room. The hotel protested that this was their "Baby sitting service," where one could get the hotel to monitor your room while you and your wife slipped down to eat at their restaurant. Hum, I should have brought a wife.

Another time running this big project across China, the negotiation turned out to be talking about two different products. While the Chinese version of the tender said "two-wheel drive" Jeeps, the English version said "four-wheel drive." I had wanted vets to be able to drive out to farmers and treat their cattle while the local directors wanted town cars for them to use, so had to get the price down.

In other instances, one side seems to be rushing the negotiations beyond what would be an expected speed. Perhaps they know something you don't?

Watch if outside people are supporting the other side. A simple ploy is where at a street stall, a tout comes along and raves over a product pretending to buy to induce a sale. This can have commercial adaptations.

(xiv) Set the meeting point

To get the best out of a negotiation it should be, as far as possible, on your terms although not obviously evident. If you have this option of setting the locale, you need to figure out whether you want the other side to be comfortable or otherwise. You can try and humor them in a nice holiday location as politicians always seem to do, and they can treat that as a holiday and become more receptive. Otherwise if your intention is to get them dealing quickly and get out of there, discomfort is one way of doing so.

The converse is for your side to feel at home within the negotiation surroundings. It is not a good idea to walk in cold when dealing with other people who might feel at home with their surroundings. It is a good idea at meetings in unfamiliar surroundings to arrive early and explore the terrain. In buildings, it's possible to review the occupant register to see who else is in the building. If this is relevant, how many floors do they take up?

Remember judges in English courts like to wear gown and wigs, which, while they will protest this is in order to protect historic convention, could also be seen as it was initially intended to intimidate everyone else in court. Translated, this could mean whether one drives up to a meeting in a Rolls-Royce or a VW, in a suit or jeans.

(xv) Set agenda

Try to make the meeting time early, leaving time for sightseeing and recreation if applicable in order to get the other side keen to complete the negotiations early.

Look at numbers of people attending meetings as too many can create negotiating problems.

Arrange if one needs to consider Jet lag, bad for your side, good if they suffer.

Who is looking into the outside light?

Adjustment of heating such as when people are not accustomed to too hot or cold.

Adjust breaks in meeting.

Arrange interjections from outside, calls to telephone, or important issues. Alternatively, arrange not to be interrupted if this is suitable.

Consider cultural issues (Ramadan, food choice).

Overall, just be careful that setting the agenda as with setting the meeting location does not come across as one concession on their part.

(xvi) Anchoring

At times, it is advantageous to get in first and set your starting position. You establish the bottom-line and the other side then have to move you from there. This would be normal where, for example, you are offering a franchise and certain conditions are to be the same for everyone. Parts of this can still be negotiated around, but the basic ground rules laid out at the start can make these nonconfrontational and the negotiations can move on.

(xvii) Socialize

Before commencing negotiations with another party, it is often useful to socialize in some form or other so that each side can feel comfortable with the other while at the same time seeking out any particular strengths or weaknesses. One however needs to be careful with this approach as it works both ways and it is well known that some people try and compromise the other side in order to gain negotiation points.

It is handy to talk about family issues, wives, and children, although even this can have some negatives if someone had split up with a partner, but currently this is so common it really does not become a major issue. Then there are of course hobbies or sports and other points of interest. Most people have or have had sporting interests. This is a good time to seek out hidden agendas. It can also be time to look at body language, whether the other side is at ease or not.

In some countries it is fairly common for ladies of the night to suddenly turn up at your hotel as an inducement. Needless to say, it is not a good idea to get involved, just as where drinking binges can have unfortunate outcomes.

(xviii) Physical presentation

Often overlooked is the physical presentation of you or your team when entering negotiations. Rule one, if in doubt it is better to overdress than turn up in singlet and shorts.

Going to my first important Ministry of Finance meeting in Bangladesh, I had been told by a colleague who had worked there that the president had decreed that to save on aircon costs, men should stop wearing silly European ties. I had really wanted to fit in and do the right thing but went wearing a tie anyway. Walking into the room all the other men were wearing ties.

There is also the question of body language. And the need to radiate a good first impression.

In the first instance, other than dress there is general demeanor. A friendly face helps as does a solid handshake. Further then in nonverbal communication, silent messages can be given on disdain such as with sitting back and folded arms. The same applied to buttoned coats.

(xix) Media

As with the comment, "Never tell a lie because it will come back to bite you," be very circumspect when dealing with the media. Even a "No" can be translated into a "Yes" by the media.

One time in Tasmania as I was close to the development manager of Gordon Barton's Tjuringa Securities, which owned Wrest Point, Australia's first legal Casino, I had a group who wanted to open another one in Launceston. This journalist had been in Sydney and someone at Tjuringa had made some reference and the journo fronted me for a comment. I said "No," which he wrote up as a "Yes," embarrassing our syndicate where one member had just posted a loss for the year. When I complained I was told the way I said NO obviously meant YES. So always watch the press even if they can be a necessary evil.

The big issue and madness over these issues currently is that with instant communications and Internet posts, this sort of material goes out instantaneously and you have no way of knowing the extent of people who might have received the information so that a retraction might not be effective.

Watch out also for the current political correctness in vogue where one needs to tread lightly on sexist, racist, and religious interpretation.

One time after the sinking of the Japanese fishing boat, Nissan Maru No. 8 off Southern Tasmania, with 22 lives lost and one Japanese only rescued, the press were hounding the poor guy for opinions. The Mercury paper wanted to fly him back to Pedra Blanca where his friends had died, the last thing the poor guy wanted. I had him billeted with our Japanese interpreter and the Mercury went ballistic with an editorial attacking our company as agents for "keeping this man from returning to pay his respects to his dead comrades." At our own subsequent Board Meeting I was chastised by the directors for letting this bad publicity get out. I picked up the phone and called the Mercury editor putting him on speakerphone in front of the Board. When I challenged his editorial, his reply was, "You can't let the facts stand in the way of a good story." I told him the whole Board had just heard him say that. We had a retraction the next day and I never had a problem with the paper again.

Currently the world is faced with another media issue, the Trump show, with a whole new approach to hard-line negotiating.

Having posted on www.the-newshub.com in September 2015 why Trump would be the next U.S. president as the first journalist to go with an endorsement while everyone else was still saying he had no show of even getting to nomination, I explained just why this would come about.

The campaign had been an illuminating illustration of negotiating techniques, on the one hand employing all the tricks of the trade, while on the other end winning by going against all the constraints of political correctness.

Start with someone having a bit of money behind him and marketing expertise. He identifies that a large part of his electorate has been dissociated from the mainstream political process and are pissed off by it. Having no previous political experience, he proceeds on the assumption that, win or lose, he builds the Trump brand name and as such, any cost is deductible. So go for broke: make outrageous comments on what people worry about.

He starts by ignoring those who he knows would not vote for him anyway; so, no need to be politically correct. Attack the other side, which is not too hard, since *no political party ever wins an election, the other side loses.*

So, how exactly does one answer his outrageous comments in the negotiation from the other side? Here is someone who can get away with it all but just what do you say when a person brings up Obama's birth certificate again, or implies his running mate had something to do with Kennedy's assassination? And one must still balk at the concept of building a wall between the United States and Mexico, allegorical perhaps but then to add "And make Mexico pay for it." This was symbolic at the time and gained people's attention but later after having won the nomination, he calms the rhetoric by a visit with the Mexican president.

How again does one respond to someone who says we need *Global Warming*, "Because its freezing and snowing in New York?" One could say, "What sort of planet is this man on?" One who boast of such a high IQ? It's all entertainment. He goes on that Hilary not being able to satisfy her husband could not satisfy America, has people bashed who throw tomatoes, advocates shooting people, and stopping ALL Muslims from coming into the country; and still gets away with it. Then on the creepy side, to make suggestions that he would like to have intimate relations with his daughter Ivanka if she wasn't his daughter and makes various references to his penis, all good stuff for possibly red necks sipping bootleg whiskey (he likes the poorly educated), but for the most powerful man on the planet?

All of this is part of a special negotiating technique. Sexist, racist, arrogant, and the list can go on, but the votes speak for themselves. And here's the rub. The frightening thing about Trump in the White House is the people who put him there. Yes, one can agree on the need to get over the political correctness that is strangling the planet and conceding that no party wins an election, the incumbents lose, but this can go a little overboard if someone keeps playing to domestic audiences. If you want to be politically incorrect, it's just as easy for others to play the game and note that what is transpiring is reaction politics. As Hitler showed us, this can be dangerous when people feel they have had enough of same/same going nowhere.

The Second World War, really an extension of WWI coupled with resentment against the perceived biased Versailles treaty and war reparations, was used by Hitler to unify the population. Once on side, the people followed despite the logic, so the comparison can be made with the blind following of Trump while not knowing which direction this will be going. This is not to imply in any way a similarity between Hitler and Trump's long-term objectives, but there are similarities in negotiation style.

Before even Trump's nomination there was little beyond inane press coverage on trivia which makes for entertaining copy but from Trump, given that so much cannot be taken seriously (distraction), there is no way anyone could tell what he really thought (keeping all options open). Was he really going to send in massive ground troops to tackle ISIS, would he roll back a deal with Iran, invade North Korea, and what would be his reaction when China finally moves to annex Taiwan? All rather serious questions.

These are the basic negotiation elements we can examine, which were attached to Trump's elephant in the room and his refusal to release tax details, important because, unlike a usual politician who has a job to show an income and investments that detail identifiable returns, to be really wealthy one has to work the system that uses whatever is legal even if it could be seen morally reprehensible, such as buying up losses. Or to minimize tax by making losses on the one hand to improve performance from another. A really successful multimillionaire can make sure that very little tax is paid and, of course, Trump falls into that category. Would anyone think he would not have employed blind trusts or have overseas accounts in tax havens routing earnings through tax-free jurisdictions?

The problem is that at least 95 percent of the voters probably don't have the money enough to take advantage of not paying tax and when after he diffused the issue for a while and the public found out what he had paid, it all went away. Trump, being the expert on throwing "dead cats on the table" to redirect attention.

All of these ploys Trump knows. What he does is a brilliant example of negotiation and the utilization of the media to achieve your ends by keeping people entertained. Most people remember, "You're fired!"

2. Phase Two: How to Debate

(i) Negotiation is like a debate with different rules

If we talk about negotiation, we really deal with two sides debating toward an outcome, except that unlike in a formal debate, there is no chairperson.

In formal debating, there is a question or a proposition (the Olympic movement has lost its purpose); one side must speak for the positive and the other the negative. Sometimes, such as in the legal question, answer YES or NO, "Have you stopped beating your wife yet?" there is no answer. Or the one side is obvious, while on the other it is difficult to justify. In negotiation, however, there are overall clear objectives where one person wants something from another.

Yet, in all negotiation, you make your points as in any debate. You start with preliminaries as when two boxers face each other in the ring. One side starts by making a pitch; so when planning, make your points and set them down.

Point 1

Point 2

Then when it's your turn again, build around each of your points while diminishing the value of the argument on the other side. In between points, there is a "filler" to keep the conversation going. In a debate, there is a time limit for each point, which usually does not exist in negotiation.

If a point is not understood it is always possible in negotiation to go back and clarify. This is particularly important if dealing between different languages.

(ii) After both sides have made their points, clarify, agree or disagree

In a debate, you have what the question is before the panel. In negotiation "We are buying THAT car," I want to buy and you want to sell.

- Try and approach the issues and not personalities.
- Avoid threats.

- Agree, but can always say—"Yes I agree, but there is that other issue." Keep the conversation going.
- Use questions rather than YES or NO.

It is then possible to use all the techniques as outlined further in this text.

(iii) To and FRO of debate

The debate in negotiation continues with the arguments back and forth on the merits or demerits of what is under consideration until an agreement is reached by both the sides. It may be that a car is for sale at a set price delivered at a set date with transfer documents and a payment of a price in a manner agreed. There can always be extras, extended warranty, time payment, and so on.

Good examples follow the matrimonial route, where couples look at deciding either where to go for a holiday or when to build a house. On planning for a holiday, partner A might just want to lay in the sun on a beach with the occasional cold beer and not have to think about anything. The holiday would be inexpensive and stay in the country. Partner B wants a holiday in Italy seeing and ticking off all the sites from Trieste through Venice, Florence, and Rome, then through to Naples in the South. You can see how this is going. A is certainly not going to get away in negotiation with an inexpensive holiday but can negotiate the cost down with a visit to just a place or two on the argument that they should be seen properly and there might just be a beach to lay on. It is unlikely A would also get away with the location being local, but perhaps it could be switched to some place NICE locally, which might incorporate a visit to one of B's friends. Or there could be a delay in an overseas visit this year to doing it properly next year.

In exchange, B could offer incentives in exchange for that position, allowing golfing or fishing weekends if A concedes, or the offer of something more personal delivered at an opportune moment. The negotiations will continue until such time that an agreement is reached. They can seek out different places online or consult travel agents; although from A's perspective, travel agents will be there to sell and his idea of a spot on the beach might end up a long way from home. Finally, a point has to be reached where both A and B can accept the compromise while perhaps not thrilled by the outcome. Beyond that, in negotiation, there might be events that can be used to derail the compromise agreement. Perhaps someone can be sick, a relative who needs attention, or some unforeseen financial expense can emerge, or it is too late to book the flights.

Of course, that is how this normally works since one must live with that partner. In real-life negotiation, and not what the books tell you, one party always wants to come out in front. The argument goes, "There is no reward for second." You either win an election or lose.

In the house building exercise, party A wants a single-level sprawling, simple design, while party B wants multilevel construction similar to something their friend has. Again, they have fairly different ideas on what they want and the price they should have to pay for it. Builders and architects can be brought in as partial mediators explaining that some options might be unworkable or too expensive within the budget. Again, at the end of the negotiation, it is likely a compromise will be reached as the negotiations go backward and forward.

(iv) Distractions

If a debate is seemingly going in the wrong direction, it is sometimes useful to offer some distraction. It can also be called going off on a side issue.

The foreign minister of Norway was having a luncheon meeting with her Tanzanian counterpart. While she was in the middle of an intense discourse on how although she found the country and the people delightful, the human rights situation was intolerable, the Tanzanian minister interrupted and pointed at a nearby tree said, "See, that is a mango tree." He stopped her dead.

Asked to take over the EU's largest project across China, which had stalled after two earlier team leaders had been sacked on being unable to deliver, I was summonsed to Brussels to be quizzed on why I thought I could do better. I was immediately put down by the commissioner saying we didn't need the project anyway and the Chinese didn't want environmental equipment. Why would I be able to make that job better? I noticed pictures of sailing yachts all around his wall and recognized one of the 72-foot Anaconda. I said that if you'd ever skippered a yacht of 16 crew in a gale with half the people seasick and still come through, you could handle anything. And I mentioned that I'd beaten Anaconda on my Desanna at the start of the

China Sea race a few years back. The rest of the time was spent talking yachting and I got the job.

At the conclusion of a debate, it is summarized and a winner declared; in a straight-out negotiation, the agreement is summarized and legalized in some form. In the case of a vehicle sale, it is the transfer of the registration and the payment for the vehicle.

Distractions that can be interposed in another form are as in department stores where intentionally the floor plans are set up so that it is easier to get in than out, the idea being of course to keep the customer shopping by distracting them from their intention of leaving. Similarly, in grocery stores, Coles, Woolworths, and the like, the everyday items people need such as milk are at the far end of the store, forcing people to pass by other items they might impulse buy.

(v) Hostage negotiations

Handling hostage situations can be a book of its own, but the basic principles remain the same, except in life-and-death situations the outcomes can be deadlier. This was found in the recent Sydney Lindt Café siege, where a "Man [Mad] Haron Monis" held 18 people hostage, which led to two deaths. The months of inquest held later highlight many of the rights and wrongs of negotiating techniques.

- Lack of homework. "Mad" Monis was out on bail on a murder charge and left walking around having previously also made threats. No one knew if he had bombs nor had anyone tried to find out. Police had sold off their response vehicle. No police had ever handled a similar situation before.
- Lack of communication. The police stopped direct negotiation with Mad Monis when he was inside while he was prepared to talk to a radio commentator.
- The terrorist chose the time and place.
- No trade. The police did not give Monis an opportunity to trade anything in exchange for publicity.
- Secondary advice. They did not call in the trained army experts to take over the operation.

- Lost opportunity. They did not use a sniper to shoot Monis although they had the opportunity.
- Lack of support. The police commissioner and assistant commissioner went home for the night during the siege.
- Poor Close. They stormed the café only after one person had been shot. The police used hard-nosed ammunition, which fractured and killed one hostage, Katrina Dawson. They fired too many times.

Overall, the situation was not well handled if evaluated against normal negotiating techniques, where the number one thing apart from him not being out on bail would have been to engage Monis in debate. Instead, they prevented him from talking to anyone, even the talk show host Ray Hadley he wanted to contact, and then allowed him to get frustrated until he cracked at 2 a.m. One terrorist. How long did they think he could stay awake before something had to give? It was failure to look at the big picture.

On a global basis with terrorist negotiations and kidnap operations, governments espouse the mantra "No negotiation with terrorists," which is designed to discourage kidnappers searching after deep pockets. In reality, hostage release negotiations continue and money changes hands but is outsourced to insurance companies specializing in this thing. By going commercial, the kidnappers know there are financial limits to their demands under insurance and so they can be more reasonable. On the other hand, where no insurance exists, governments can still keep their hands seemingly clean but using insurance companies as an intermediary front. Again, with the addition of continually seeking "proof of life" from kidnappers, all the standard negotiation techniques apply.

(vi) Always come away with something

While a fairly simple concept, at the end of a negotiation it should always be designed to have achieved something, at worst a lesson learned. And if you are selling, just make it easy for people to give you money.

3. Phase Three: How to Propose

(i) In proposals there are either competing or compatible wants

In proposals, whether commercial or domestic, negotiation is simplified if both sides want the same thing, for example, to sell a car and to buy a car; or to get married. This understanding is however time contingent, meaning that the proposal to sell the car and the intention to buy the car might not last if the warranty has run out. The same with marriage.

A useful analogy on proposals is through human courtship where we try and have compatible wants. These can be for completely different reasons but aimed in the end at a marriage or a partnership.

(ii) Compatible is when both sides have the same agreement

In this situation where both sides are already in agreement, that makes the negotiation easier, but too easy an agreement can lead to mistakes being made; like buying an Alfa Romeo at a very good price to later find it had been driven on European salted roads and the bottom was rusting out.

If back to the courtship analogy, both sides can be moving toward agreement, but one still has to be careful that this is for all the right reasons and you finish up with exactly what you want. As with the buying of the car, you might only discover the defects later when it is too late or proves too expensive to run. The car looked good in the showroom but not that great out on the road.

The Blue Lotus Europa my friend lent me while overseas looked like a great car, so low slung you actually lay behind the wheel and boy did it go. I could get below the boom gate at the airport car park. The problem was then getting hit at a roundabout because the oncoming car could not see me behind the shrubbery. Careful what you wish for.

(iii) Competing is when there are differences

In the example quoted in regard to the car, the overall aims are the same but there remains the issue of price. The seller wants as much as they can and at least to cover their base costs as a minimum and the buyer also wants it at the least cost.

On our marriage/partnership scenario, all of the negotiation factors come into play. The two parties want a union, but one side may want security. There would be perhaps differences on numbers of children desired, if any; where they might want to live and compatible ways of earning a living. And always consider the elephant in the room of a prenuptial agreement.

We start with individuals putting themselves in the market place with the offer of a relationship. They chose the location where they will negotiate, at work, in the gym, or at a nightclub, or in bed. The locations we chose are where we are most comfortable and where it is most likely for us to deal with compatible types.

Each individual is then competing with others to land a specific agreement for the relationship and will be having to negotiate toward a conclusion. One man could be using (offering) his attractive appearance as part of his offered negotiation, his personality, his social position, numbers of friends, and how they see him, or the quality and type of car. The other side, in this case, the woman looks at these offerings and values them for what she wants or thinks she wants and evaluates them against what else is available in the market. If eventually the offer meets all of her criteria, she will ACCEPT the OFFER and a union is CLOSED.

As indicated earlier, from there all the legal issues come into play, but these really have little bearing on the negotiation techniques other than if that prenuptial agreement to be signed was part of the negotiation process.

(iv) State what the proposal is then stop talking

When one has stated the offer of what is proposed, stop talking. STOP. Some people become over keen to finalize a deal that they keep on trying to sell and in some cases talk themselves out of the win.

Everyone is likely to have experienced the salesman who keeps on and on trying to sell you, while you are trying to decide which model you want. Instead of letting you get on with it in the quiet of your own mind, their chatter becomes really irritating and in the end you walk away and go to another store.

Within our matrimonial example the same applies. If you are trying too hard to win her favor, she is just as likely to think that it's all too much. They have written hundreds of songs illustrating what can happen. Give it a rest, BUT there is nothing to stop you coming back later.

(v) If that does not work, consider alternative proposals

If the overall deal falls through, consider alternative proposals. As a very wise old man once said, "If the deal isn't exactly what you want move on and the next one will be better."[1]

Similarly, if that girl did not work out, perhaps it was meant to be, but there is surely one perhaps better around the corner. In case you don't believe this, look back at some past girlfriends and see how that worked out.

If they won't buy a Mercedes, try a Lexus, a Toyota, a Mazda, or if none of this works, try selling them a Holden or a Ford.

---

[1] My father, when I couldn't buy the first sports car I wanted.

4. Phase Four: Bargaining

(i) Bargaining involves making exchanges

Life is one long bargaining session, from the cradle to the grave. We give up something for something else. Globally, the child eats the vegetables so that they can watch TV. The child cleans their room so they can go to play with a friend. The child believes in religion because they are told to. A person gives up some freedom to get married in exchange for companionship and in response to the biological urge to have children. The real consideration becomes whether what is given up compensates for what one receives in return.

In negotiation, both the sides win if each gets exactly what they want or reasonably expect. It is like a swing between A winning with all of what they want against B winning very little of what they want. That is what bargaining is all about, give and take, and a swing between the two positions. The reality in negotiation is that you want it to swing your way.

(ii) All bargains should be conditional

Following on from the need to have two sides to a bargain, there should not be anything given away for nothing. There can be small gestures to show goodwill; but in that case, the goodwill should be obvious and appreciated.

In the case of the Lake Gordon flooding and having to save some of the timber, the government policy was that no untreated timber products could be exported from Australia. There had to be value added at home as sawn timber or woodchips. The conditionality that finally allowed the government to give their approval was that this was a once off or otherwise considerable revenue would be lost for nothing.

In the mid-1980s, the EU was trying to sell China its airplanes as against the U.S. Boeing. As a sweetener, they wanted to offer China a project grant, so they came up quickly with a 60 million euro dairy development project.

In our domestic scenario, we have that intimacy is conditional to at least an "engagement," if not a marriage.

(iii) Nothing should be given away for free

Working on the adage "There is no such thing as a free lunch," it follows that nothing should be given away for free in a negotiation. The main issue is that backing away from a starting position can be seen as a weakness and leads to demands for even greater concessions.

A difficult position arose since one particular good journalist friend would never let me pay for lunch even though we enjoyed each other's company and I could have written it off as a business expense. He argued that one day he might have to write something negative about me or one of my interests and so did not want to be beholding for that lunch. I could never quite understand that, and could not really tell him my reward was already having his brilliant wife joining us for that lunch. Then perhaps he was right!

Sometimes when trying something for free it works against you.

During the fun times at Sydney University where I was advertising manager for the student magazine "honi soit," Richard Neville decided to set up OZ Magazine and run excerpts from "Lady Chatterley's" Lover as a confrontation to the censorship laws. In fact, we would have been happy to give this paper away free just to stick it to the establishment, but I suggested a higher price that allowed the newsagents to make 20c an issue, which was at the time way above what any other news sheet provided. Oz went like hot cakes.

The interchange about nothing for free works around, "If you do this then I do that."

In negotiation, it revolves around *quid pro quo,* made clear when there are concessions.

(iv) Don't underestimate the personal

People dealing with governments and companies often overlook the personal side in the negotiation equation. If a potential recruit fronts to McDonalds and says their life's ambition is to cook potato chips at Maccers, who would believe them? If they say they want to work there to learn their marketing strategy and is prepared to fry while doing so, one could believe and support them. One such fryer I know started at McDonalds Thornleigh in Sydney to go on to be a leading Chef in London.

If a person is coming to work for you, a manager should have some idea of people's personal agenda. Are they grateful for the work or just needing a Job; is this just seen as a stepping stone to a better job; are they looking at setting up in competition? Many "How to negotiation books" suggest one should separate people from the problem, but is that really true?

If an accountant in a company is told they have to hire an assistant, can you be sure the right candidate would be selected, who may later become a threat to the accountant? The same with hiring people older than the recruiter; in which case, the recruiter may feel threatened. What happens when you have a negotiation team and someone in the team does not want its leader to succeed? People will often go to great lengths for job security.

The personal problem is a major issue since in EVERY large organization there exist personality classes, either obvious or hidden. These can be envy over work levels, over salary, or just personality conflicts. These can work in your favor if you can identify them from the other side but can be disastrous for your own if not recognized. From your end, you can play "Good Cop Bad Cop" as long as it's an act. If the tactic is employed, it helps to switch roles from time to time. Part of this system alludes to "Of course I would love to help but it's the other guy."

Jim Nichols was the best rural property salesman I've ever known. Having been crippled during the Second World War he argued that he didn't know how long he'd live, so he had to provide for his children. We used to go out to buy farms. The front gate would come off in his hand. His foot would go through the timber on the porch. He would accidently find fault with every-thing while I played "Good Cop." Then we'd switch and again, until the seller was so confused they'd agree to our offer and we'd have a deal.

The bottom-line in entering negotiations is to assume that everyone will have their own agenda (as demonstrated in the following practical sessions) and be on the lookout for them. From your own team you should have some idea where people are coming from in your own pecking order, but this may not be as obvious from the other side. The secret is to be able to pull everyone's agendas in the same direction so that individuals win within the overall plan. This is not only about personal goals but also applies collectively to group goals.

My first driver in Africa Fusi, was given five dollars to put oil in the car. He spent the money on himself, the car ran out of oil, the engine seized, and the car was destroyed. He no longer had a job, but had gained $5 while I had no car.

Remember that people generally do not like making other people uncomfortable, which can work both for you or against you.

(v) Shifting position

Sometimes when things are not going well, it is necessary to shift position. Typical car salesman's ploy is downsizing if they feel the customer can't afford the better car. The switch could of course be in the other direction and can also be done intentionally. First, one model is shown and then out comes the whizzbang better version. The salesman's inference is then, "But of course this would be too expensive for you."

It may also be advantageous to move from a BUY to a LEASE. If they don't want to sell you that hotel, a lease might show a better return after you do the sums. Restaurants as the second most-likely businesses to go bankrupt in Australia after owner-operated truck drivers would be a good example of what to be careful of when investing. Homework.

You can also rotate the people if a person on your team seems to be annoying the other side to your disadvantage. In that case, replace them. If the annoyance is helping you, keep them in. The same applies for annoying people on the other side, although it is probably harder for you to get them to replace their own people.

What you can do is shift the ground around how and when you negotiate.

Early on in dealing with the Japanese, in daylong meetings they would rotate their people every hour or so while I had to sit there without a break. I did not want to seem rude, but in the end I called a halt and told them that if any of their people had to step out for a break, I'd take that opportunity myself. They stopped.

(vi) Sacrifice

Sometimes in a negotiation as in a game of chess, it is necessary to sacrifice something of yours in order to gain a larger advantage. In the most extreme case, you lose one soldier to save many.

In day-to-day negotiations, one might have to give up on one deal, to show good faith or to cement future relations, or to live to fight another day. As a bottom-line, no sacrifice should be made unless there is something to be gained from it, unless the gain is to confuse them. If the other side will never deal with you again or hostages are shot anyway, it is not much use making the sacrifice.

In an army officer theoretical training exam, we were given a scenario for an important hill we had to capture with our platoon of 30 men. My submitted solution was for a small diversion attack from the rear and then front and flank up the center. Casualty, one by accident. I was failed. On complaining, I was told that we had been told that it was an IMPORTANT hill and so it should have been an assault straight up the guts. Allowance 30 percent casualty rate.

(vii) Third party intervention

Historically, in some societies, marriage brokers have been employed. Apart from using an expert to find suitable economic and family ties for a couple, face can be saved if the other side rejects a suitor. It also helps where culturally young people are not meant to mix freely so would not have much choice.

Consequently, in all negotiations, a third party can be brought in to speed up or smooth things along. An outsider to the transaction can help things along when bringing in a well-known or famous person. This is done sometimes when leaders bring in their predecessors to make a point, but this is not always a good idea since these people out of the limelight can say too much.

Remembering the saying, "Someone who decides to defend themselves in court has a fool for a client," often an expert in a situation can bring with them advice which can be helpful. This can be as part of the negotiation team or sitting apart and consulted from time to time.

(viii) Ploys

Added to shifting positions could be some other avenues with which to switch the negotiation your way by unsettling the other side. These include, not in order:

(a) False starting position

A typical example most people have experienced would be where a sales person first starts to offer an inferior product when what they intend to sell you is something more expensive.

In a commercial setting, this would include adding additional features you have never considered.

Buying my first new Mercedes-Benz from the factory in Rome after joining the UN, I was in this office of a very suave sales lady who reminded me of Letitia from the Adam's Family. I knew exactly what I wanted, a 300D Mercedes and the catalogue had told me the price. She said, "Of course you do." She then told me I would of course want alloy wheels. That was $500 a wheel extra. I wanted to ask whether they didn't come with wheels. Then I had to have a Mexicana stereo system and of course a sliding sunroof. By the time she finished with me, I had added 30 percent to the catalogue price.

Actually, she did me a favor, since later selling it in Africa to an Indian merchant, only "fully loaded" vehicles had a market and I got back my buying price.

(b) Holding back

While it is best to never tell a lie, one has to remember you don't have to always tell the whole story. We all know the car that is bought and then the wheels fall off. There are some consumer laws that give some recourse to buyers who have been duded, but overall, it's really about "Buyer beware."

Selling my old yacht, which did have some problems but not serious enough to highlight, when asked if it could sail around the world, my reply "Well its sailed on five major overseas yacht races and could do so again" was not a lie. That it needed a good crew to achieve this did not have to be added since it should be a taken.

From this, the mantra should still remain never lie but just be careful how you present the truth.

If you sell some things such as a gun, you need to ensure that the buyer is appropriately licensed to buy and own it. One can generally assume that if licensed, they know how to use it.

(c) Setting preconditions

Sometimes one side or the other can set preconditions to the negotiations. This would be fairly common in negotiating for a franchise where they are unlikely to change standard conditions just for you; unless of course you are a big enough customer. Dominant players such as Coca-Cola won't make concessions and McDonalds used not to, but are now a little more flexible if the money is right.

I negotiated with McDonalds for the first franchise in Albania on behalf of a major potato farmer who thought this would provide a good market for his crop. Unfortunately, Maccers insisted on one type of potato he did not produce and so we had no deal.

Currently, we have Apple in such a dominant industry position that it can lead a market and simply bring out a new phone and say, "Take it or leave it." That even when the next model has no major new features one couldn't be without. They can even change models, so you no longer use old ear pieces/phones and have to buy their new ones. There nevertheless are other options.

(d) Changing venues and times midstream

Bringing on change can be a good move if negotiations are stalemated or not really going anywhere. Hitting the fire alarm button may not be a good way to achieve this, but there can be any number of excuses. These can include someone being taken ill, a lead negotiator being called away, the venue rental expiring, and anything else creative.

If stalemated negotiations are the problem, you don't lose anything by changing location, whereas, for example, if you survive the fire, both sides have something in common and perhaps that will assist negotiations.

When I bought the famed "Ball & Chain" restaurant in Hobart for the company to convert to a Japanese Seamen's Club, I told the MD that before we started renovations I wanted to use it and its internal rotisserie for a lunch I'd like to give my friends. Unfortunately, my colleague Ian Bampton I'd talked into doing one of his famous sheep on the spit, got carried away with the kindling and the sheep was engulfed in flames. The fire got up into the flue, which with years of grease caught as well, the ceiling went, the second-floor welds melted and by the time I got to the fourth floor that too was on fire. I opened the window and called for a fire brigade just as my guests were arriving. My friends certainly got some good pictures for the front page of the Mercury newspaper the next day and we adjourned to my waterfront house at Howrah with a charred sheep. The aftermath was that the MD chastised me on Monday for damage to the building. Sadly, I had to explain that we would have had to gut the building anyway and now the insurance would have to pay for it. He said he didn't want to hear any more. And the ABC gave me a weekly spot on TV after the news.

(e) Having intimidating venues

Not suggesting venues on Mt. Everest or Mt. Qogir (K2) as the most intimidating but some others can put you off your lunch.

In Korea, one of the worst was sitting in a beautiful rural setting awaiting lunch when we saw this man with a hessian bad smashing its contents on the concrete. This went on for a while until I asked what he was doing. Only to be told he was beating a dog to death as it tenderized this for our lunch. It's hard to know what to say.

Another venue in NE China had us sitting out looking at two tigers in a cage at the bottom of the lawn. Finishing lunch there was a lot of chatter with the staff until one of the waiters emerged with a live rabbit, taking it down and dropping it into the tiger's cage. The tigers toyed with the rabbit for a while before chomping it, much to the delight of the lunch crowd. More excited talk and some money changed hands with the manager. My table had another round of drinks. Along came this waiter leading a mangy old cow, which he shoved mooing into the tiger cage. We had to sit there while they slowly munched it to death amid the cheers of the audience.

Some intimidating venues can be where traditionally drinking becomes part of the negotiations. All over China and in particular on the NW frontier bordering on Russia, in Albania, and other parts of eastern Europe, it is quite normal to be welcomed with some strong drink at 10 a.m., which can just be the start to a day's long negotiation session. Sometimes it is not possible to avoid negotiating in these areas, but at other times, it is impossible to avoid these sessions.

Working on distributing donor grants in the aforementioned areas, this required going to remote locations and evaluating project proposals prior to signing off on the payments. Obviously, people about to receive thousands in donations try very hard to be hospitable but do this is in the only way they know with drinking just a part of this. For them it might be only be just one special occasion but was not fun when repeated day after day.

(f) Declaring some issues nonnegotiable

Nonnegotiable issues can be good if they work. It is possible to say that you will not negotiate if bribes have to be paid but it is still difficult to say that upfront, in danger of it being taken as an insult. It is far easier to stipulate that we need to work within government guidelines and imply that these will be followed (whatever they are). This commonly applies in awarding franchises where certain basic principles apply to every franchisee.

(g) Switching

Then there is moving from traditional gaining something for nothing, to getting something for something or to where both sides win. As in the seesaw, you keep switching around to blindside the opposition.

In Tasmania, the apple growers had just lost the UK market and some turned to oyster farming. The Pacific oyster was twice as big as the famed Sydney Rock Oyster but grew in half the time. Problem was no one knew the Pacific oyster, and everyone just wanted the Sydney Rock. I came up with a similar box packaging for the Tasmanian oyster, calling it GEM Brand, and set off to the mainland with a box of each type. None of the main hotels would even try these oysters until at the Hilton in Adelaide the chef spat out the Pacific oyster he tried. This really annoyed me, so had a think about it and two months later went straight back to the chef in Adelaide. First, he tried the oyster from the SYDNEY box and then again spat out the oyster from the GEM box. When I explained to him that I had switched boxes on him to prove his bias, he immediately ordered 40 dozen GEM brand and since then the Pacific oyster has not looked back on the Australian market.

Another form of switching can be when a purpose can be modified. Unwanted churches or firehouses can be used for other purposes such as houses, galleries, or restaurants.

Farmers had invested in the local abattoir in Hobart, Tasmania, and it was in danger of being shut down because of lack of throughput. I was simply told to come up with an idea to save it. Doing my homework, I found that under "Muslim kill," or halal preparation, once the slaughter has taken place the premises have to be "cleansed" and cannot be used for the rest of the day. All the abattoirs on the mainland available for this were too large for what amounted to halal treatment since they could not then just shut down for the rest of the day. Our abattoir was just the right size and they flew down a guy from Melbourne once a week to administer the necessary blessings.

Switching can also be used in order to get out of a situation. One horrible case was with the company, The Sydney Blood Bank Ltd. The idea was that in *light of the AIDS scare, you donated your own, presumably safe blood, and the Blood bank stored it for you in case you ever needed it. The accountants who handled the float received preference share options as did the law firm handling the legal work. The manager of the blood bank then stupidly came out with some statement of how he could now clean all blood of contamination, so you could get his company to clean it for you. The shares went from around $2 to $18 at a peak before the Stock Exchange shut down trading. Meanwhile, however, the accounting and law firms had exercised their 20c options and cashed out near the top, making a fortune in the process. They then had the problem of what to say when the investigation started, since while technically their actions were legal, it did not have a good look to it. Next minute the manager was suddenly arrested on theft charges. When I later checked, the theft was that he had not returned his neighbor's ride-on lawn mower.*

Negotiation very often involves **Thinking outside the box.**

(h) Disdain for another's products

It is possible to put others into discomfort by implying that the products you are negotiating to buy are badly inferior to what you really want, you will take them anyway, but at a lower price. Possibly not a good way to win friends and influence people. It can however work if it is true. The rejoinder is of course, "Then go and buy theirs."

The same applies not just to products but also to proposals. The disdain by comparison here is that you pull apart each layer of what they are offering and refer to some other model that might be better. "Your car does not have reversing camera, the GPS comes out of the dash and is not built in, the wheels are not alloy, and so on." The same thing can work if you are implying that they will not do a good job with your franchise and so will have to pay more for it than would other successful companies.

(i) Ganging up

It is possible to use others in a similar position to reinforce your own. A typical example is one where individuals or companies are forced into industry associations. "Either you join, or you do not get accreditation."

One example in serious negotiations can be when one company taking over the other can guarantee jobs in the new company for the top executives. The company employees being taken over can gang up to push a deal through. At best, this ensures that these people will not be obstructive and at best will help to ease the way. One needs to be careful here since this can border on the illegal if confidential information facilitating the takeover is supplied to secure future positions. Also, watch *Insider Trading* under these situations.

In Tasmania, Farmers and Graziers Society was taken over by Webster and Woolgrowers Ltd. and all the directors of the former were offered management position in the new company structure.

In Hong Kong, just prior to the hand back to the Mainland, working for the Hong Kong Society of Accountants, I was to look at the integration of the accounting bodies post hand back between HK, Taiwan, and China. Of course, not all three representatives could meet in the same room, so I was shuffling between them trying to find some reconciliation. It became apparent that where HK (who were paying me) had around 650 members, China had about 20,000, and there was never to be an amalgamation that HK people would accept. The only way out was for each to retain their own identity and remain friends.

(j) Blocking

In blocking, one organizes the market to shut out the competition. Supermarkets can use it where there is always competition for shelf space and usually you get on the best shelves if you accept their price or if you have a very salable product.

While setting up Weyerhaeuser's Australian company, where previously shiploads of timber had been organized by a consortium of timber merchants in Sydney, our policy became to bring in whole shiploads ourselves unloaded in Homebush Bay. The idea was to block the consortium on a five-year plan by lowering prices until the competition was out of the way, would never be able to regroup, after which prices could be increased.

(k) Salami

The technique is based on divide and conquer.

By issuing threats and in forming alliances, it attempts to overcome opposition to eventually take over. The opposition as in politics is removed as in a salami, slice by slice, until the other side realizes it is too late and that it is gone (as in the "Survivor" TV series). The system works best if true motives can be hidden. Also applied in "fifth column," activities or when one nation populates another until they dominate.

Muslim extremists in the UK are predicting that with their high birth rates and chipping away at local acceptance, they will be gradually eventually be able to introduce Sharia law: same principle.

(l) Russian front
During the Second World War, one of the biggest threats, as outlined in sitcoms, such as "Hogan's Heroes," was to be sent to the Russian Front where the fighting was at its most brutal. Hence, this technique is about offering something they will never chose as an alternative to what you offer.

Car salesmen often try and hard sell someone on a *junker* in order to sell up. They learn to read potential buyers and would say, "Look I know this Mercedes is far too expensive for someone in your position, so I would suggest this XYZ jalopy that would be more in your price bracket."

(m) Walking away
These ploys might not exactly be dirty tricks but can affect negotiations. Always remember any ploy can backfire and others may also be using ploys. If you walk away, make sure you can walk back.

One time I was head hunted by Chartered accounting firm, Lay Hart Room and Hyland for a job involving restructuring the company business to be less reliant on the wool industry. I was flown in and had to be interviewed by the holding company Board of Directors, all of whom would have been forty years my senior. During the interview in this venerable old building, it became quickly apparent that I would never get this job, reinforced when they asked me, "What do you know about timber?" They were, unbeknown to me, looking at trying to establish farmer timber coops for their client base. I had worked for the world's largest timber firm in the world, Weyerhaeuser, but that was more as an office manager and accountant. So, I said that I knew nothing about timber. When they asked for my fee rate, knowing I would not get the job, I asked for double what I was getting. Later at lunch with one of the directors, Jim Nichols, I was told I had the job at my rate. He said they were all impressed by how I handled that silly question about timber, since obviously having worked for Weyerhaeuser I would have known everything about timber and they probably had insulted me.

Do Your Homework.

(n) If at first you don't succeed, try again

While it is pointless flogging the proverbial dead horse, if you believe in something and at first you get knocked back, try again. Perhaps that will no longer work for Hillary Clinton. Remember always that on a personal level there is such a thing as a "Use by date."

A good example of persistent trying is where one of the now leading food manufacturers in Australia, Carmen's Gourmet Foods, was trying to get on the shelf in the supermarkets, Carolyn Creswell, the lady who set up and owned the business was continually knocked back. In keeping on trying, she got into a small chain but they took her products off again after a few months. It took her a year to get back there. Some years later and she is on the shelves of all the supermarket chains, she is exporting to 30 international markets and the Chinese market is far bigger than in Australia. Good success story, but how do you know when it's time to give up?

A friend of mine, now a still fit 95-year-old, made a packet on selling a speed reading improvement course franchise. He wanted, he said, to do me a favor and line up some overseas franchises from him. Looking at his material it was quite impressive as were his references, but it was all hard copy style and totally outdated in this electronic age. Hence, the answer to the question has to be around doing your research. In this case, there are many similar brilliant courses available online, which would make his system obsolete. If you look around and find so many similar products on the market, unless they all have missed an element you believe is crucial, or have an incredible amount of money to spend, it would be worthwhile looking for something else.

There are some brilliant new ideas for mousetraps out there in the market, but it's hard to see how many of these would be cost-efficient.

(ix) Mediation

A different type of ploy can involve mediation. They say a lawyer in court is a fool if asking a question to which they don't already know the answer.

Similarly, if using mediation as a ploy, it helps when thinking that going to mediation will go your way.

Mediation works through a mediator who can be either judicial or appointed by some body in an official capacity, or be an independent person agreed to by the parties. Going the legal way, there is little choice in picking the mediator so decisions can go either way, whereas in your own selection the outcome could be better. Many countries have mediation bodies such as through Chambers of Commerce, but while these bodies should have commercial knowledge and experience, don't hold your breath that a Chinese or Vietnamese mediator is going to find in favor of a foreigner.

(x) Dirty tricks

In talking about shifting positions, this opens the door to dirty tricks. These can be endless. These are defined as "unethical, duplicitous or illegal tactics employed to destroy or diminish the effectiveness of political or business opponents." In other words, they are nasty. These dirty tricks can be used in selling and or getting ahead of an opponent.

Examples:
(a) Phony information

Remember never lie, but there are many ways of telling the truth. For now, as we have seen, there is "Fake news" and it is really hard to check this out. One company now has developed an app that on a SWARM system can analyze news to come up with what is most likely to be the truth and also give left-wing and right-wing alternatives.

From your homework you should be able to work out what is real for you, but if information is otherwise suspected, no harm in displaying interest in the information presented and make them elaborate.

Real Estate Agents used to be very good at this. I remember attending one auction where I knew one of the staff of the agency who asked me to come along as an observer to make up the numbers since they said they only had one buyer from Singapore. Some guy, I suppose a plant, opened the bidding at $1.2 million and then there was a bid supposedly coming in over the phone to 1.25m, then the plant, 1.5, over the phone 1.75. The agent with the Chinese *guy then gave him a nudge and he bid 1.85m. The auctioneer knocked it down to him so quickly, the poor Singaporean guy as the only genuine bidder didn't even know what happened.*

The rules here have since changed so every bidder has to register to prove they are genuine, but it is hard to see how this can be policed. It nevertheless reinforces the need to do one's homework and if something does not appear right, STOP.

Another angle is where someone will tell you something so outrageous that people will fall for it. Do you want to buy the Sydney Harbor Bridge? Just as with the man who sold the Eifel Tower. In simpler forms, people shown what purports to be a diamond ring without exactly saying it's a diamond, asking and getting a huge price only to have it prove to be a fake.

One old scam was where someone advertised that if you sent $1 in a self-addressed, postpaid envelope, you would get the secret of how to get rich. When you sent the money, you received back instructions to do the same thing. This is covered also under straight out misleading information. Currently, the same ploy is used over the Internet. If the guy was making so much money with his scheme, why does he have to spend so much time selling it to others?

It is also possible to intentionally lead the other side off in the wrong direction. In this they are negotiating about something that is really not on the table. They might believe they are getting benefits that the other side have no intention of giving them. This is now shown in the Australian Banking Royal Commission,[1] which shows how banks and finance companies had been charging customers, including a deceased for financial advice they never provided.

(b) Assumed authority

Similar to someone asserting phony information, assuming authority they might not have can be challenged. If serious, you can suggest waiting until that person is present or a decision can be confirmed by a phone call.

---

[1] Australian Royal Commission into Misconduct in the Banking, Superannuation and Financial Services Industry, 2018.

Examples:

- With the sale of the Eifel Tower, Victor "Lustig" (German for funny), sold it not once but twice. This was at a time when French newspapers were discussing the removal of the tower, which had been intended as a temporary structure for the World Fair. Lustig went to some scrap dealers and told them that since the government wanted to keep things quiet about the sale, he had been appointed to negotiate with nominated buyers. He concluded a final deal and got a cashier's check. The final stroke of genius to convince the buyer that he was genuine was when he had asked for a minor "consideration" for assisting their firm to win the contract before accepting the check. This made them think he was genuine and he walked away with the cash. The second time he tried, he was caught.
- A pig farmer advertised that he was the owner of a large pig farm and was selling prized pigs and a purchased pig would have an ear tag with the owner's name inscribed. This went well until it was discovered that there was only one pig with some 5,000 tags attached to its ears. The farmer was never sued since he had not lied.
- A similar scam was for an app sold for £999, which did absolutely nothing. Only eight were sold before Apple pulling the app within 24 hours, but some people were taken in by something that just glowed in the middle yet had advertised in its promo that it has "no hidden functions at all."

(c) Increasing demands

Increased demands can be introduced where your side has no authority to negotiate on these. The idea is to try to force you to accept what was proposed before the extra demands.

This can be usually when the other side always intended to introduce the demands but went in low key to get your interest. This is now seen daily on the Internet with "hooks" sent out to get your interest. Scantily clad girls and puppy dogs seem to be favorites. Click on these and then someone is trying to sell you something.

To get around this, one can bluff and introduce extra demands of your own.

(d) Lock-in tactics

Lock-in tactics are those when someone gives an ultimatum such as resigning or cancelling all business if their demands are not met. It can also be when the other side demands that you only sell their product. It is of course not a dirty trick if it was known before that this is how the company deals, for example, where someone are only allowed to sell Coke or Pepsi, but it is a dirty trick when it was not on the table at the beginning.

(e) Making people uncomfortable

It is possible to set meeting locations in places that are uncomfortable. Temperature can also be regulated to put people ill at ease. Remember however if this is obvious it can backfire.

Uncomfortable feeling can also come from people speaking among themselves in their language during negotiations. This might be considered rude, but it can be a dirty trick.

A common ploy of course used for centuries from the reception desk onwards is to employ attractive young ladies to be around to offer distraction to the other side. If you star in "Suits," it is possible to finish as part of the British Royal Family.

In talking about making people uncomfortable, the arch proponent of this would have had to have been the former Lang Hancock, the then richest man in Australia, because of his mining concessions. His daughter has now taken on that role. Stories of his abrupt manner and dealings with people are legendary.

During my involvement with Hancock, no Australian bank would deal with him; so he was using New Zealand. I had to finally find a German BT bank branch agreeing to fund his McCamey Monster project. In payment for my work, Hancock had promised to cut me in for a share of royalties as he swore he would do this on his own and not sell out. Only he double-crossed me anyway by selling out to BHP, having just used me to show it was possible. When confronted over my payment, his final words to me were "Sue me."

Once while I was in Hancock's office in Macquarie Street, Sydney, he called out to his secretary to get Bjelke Joh Petersen, the premier of Queensland, on the phone. She responded shortly after, with "He's in Parliament." Hancock shouted back, "Well tell him to get his arse out of there."

Hancock could certainly make everyone around him uncomfortable.

(f) Showing lack of interest

In a take-it-or-leave-it mentality, by showing a lack of real interest in an outcome can be a way of getting what you want.

The best jobs and deals I have ever had or won were when I did not really want or need them. It's as if the casualness of approach translates into negotiating techniques. If you could bottle that, you could make a fortune. In reality, it is how one radiates confidence, which comes naturally to some and had to be learned by others.

Just remember in line with the approach outlined earlier, if at all possible, when applying for a job, already have a job. Be really desperate to get a job, while you are told that enthusiasm will win it for you, the desperation comes across and will work against you. It's like believing God is on your side.

(g) Delayed actual negotiation

This is often really more of a technique than a dirty trick but can be one when a parallel negotiation is taking place. You would know this if you were ever *gezumped* in a real estate transaction. Those on the other side are dealing with someone else but want to keep you interested while they try for a higher price. Much of this borders on the illegal but nevertheless goes on continuously, given that as in the CLOSE, no agreement is reached until said CLOSE is a final agreement. Remember estate agents do this as part of their skills set and this is why they have earned such a bad name, even if what they do remains within the law.

(h) Threats

Threats can be in relation to walking away or offered as a consequence if the other side does not comply. There can also be threats of nonpayment or that there could be retaliation on your other business interests if you don't comply. Or they will go with your main competitor.

One of the most concerning examples of threats is where, for example, major retailers can demand their suppliers accept their price or they will lose their market. The suppliers have little choice but to comply with no comeback and they can be eventually driven into bankruptcy. The only way out is to go to the media or some government body that could intervene.

Some other types of threats can be very real. There have been instances where consultants on international projects have been intimidated for not playing along with embezzlement of project donor funds, for in any way revealing corrupt practices or suggesting that they might. With this also come implied threats.

Spending an afternoon with the head of a major donor agency in a Third World country, we had time to kill and I mentioned a recent scandal where some $200 million project money had gone missing and why had his agency done nothing. He explained that he'd had head office auditors in for a few days who gave it a clear bill of health and, beyond that, if he complained to his local counterpart, there would be a complaint to his bosses and he would be recalled. Career finished because "He couldn't get on with the locals." Say nothing, finish his time, get a gong and off with a promotion.

(i) Strait our misrepresentation
Remembering the scam where someone advertised a get rich scheme asking for $10 to be sent with a self-addressed envelope and they would send you a scheme guaranteed to make you rich. The present-day version online is "I made $40,000 in a just one month. Send me $1,000 and I will send you the secret," that being of course to con 40 other people to send you $1,000.

Otherwise, some people just operate in bad faith in misrepresentation where they have no intention of going through with what they offer.

(xi) Bribery
Bribery rates in a class of its own as a dirty trick that is illegal. When it happens, it usually comes in one of two forms. One side finding something against someone on the other side and using this either directly or implied to influence an outcome, or alternatively when a situation is artificially created for a similar end. The main advice here is that don't get involved because it can always come back and bite you.

It's difficult if a past event comes up where you can't turn back the clock. Politicians particularly find this can destroy their career. Obviously, it all depends on the circumstances, but if you get set up and are caught, there are at least ways to diffuse the impact. The first is to come out with an admission that can be delivered on your own terms and own time. Trump again is an expert in this, laughing charges off, alleging "fake news" or even twisting it in his favor, making other men admire his sexual prowess.

Shifting concern to someone else's problem helps if there is something that can come up that is even bigger news than your own issue; remember the movie where they decided to invent a war to take the heat off the political issue. Trump could initiate a threat of war to distract from an alleged former relationship with a prostitute.

In the case of the manufactured "compromise," the easiest thing to say would be don't fall for it. The first DON'T is don't hunt in packs. A common practice is for a group night on the tiles that gets a little carried away and everyone thinks you're all into this together, except that it's a setup. The other side are all single and you have a wife who won't like some of the pictures.

On my first trade mission to Bangkok, we ran into an ex-dry cleaner from Ulverston in Tasmania who had moved to Bangkok, taken up he said with the Queen of Pat Pong, and owned the Pink Lotus nightclub and the Takara Massage parlor. From the diplomatic cocktail party, we adjourned with him to the Pink Lotus watching ping-pong balls fly around and then he invited everyone back to the Takara. In quick time, my ten colleagues including one very senior politician disappeared out the back with the pretty girls sitting in the foyer. I declined, so was invited back to the owner's office for a drink. Sipping good whiskey, there on a ray of TV monitors showing my colleagues hard at it in their individual rooms.

I'm not sure there was follow-up bribery in this case but there could have been, and not compromising anyone in my group but this Takara owner did not get rich so quickly selling beer. Remember also how in this day and age, everyone carried a mobile phone and any activity can finish up online circulating the globe within minutes.

Another example of bribery is in relation to winning contracts. Many people believe that this is confined to Third World settings, but it can be alive and well in the First World, only here it is more sophisticated. Typical examples are where "You do this for us and we will give you a consulting contract. You don't have to do anything for it except send us one-line reports on something once a month along with an invoice."

A leading life insurance company wanted me to use my influence as a named partner of an accounting firm to use my contacts to do business with their company. They gave me a check for $1,000,000 to put into my account and told me the ownership of the money was to remain theirs, but the interest was to be mine. When I returned their money saying no deal, I still did well on the interim interest. I will never know if they then went to another partner in our firm.

In such cases, ensure that you keep it legal and include any income in your tax returns so that it does not come back later to bite you. Remember that the tax people brought down Al Capone when no one else could get him.

In another case, I tendered a petrol supply contract for the company's pump serving our fleet of 280 vehicles. With the bids in, the manager of one company offered me a personal kickback of 5 cents a liter to award them the contract. Incensed, I went to the managing director insisting that this company be excluded even though their price had been the lowest. The billionaire MD had a different opinion and had me go back and tell the guy he had the contract, but take the 5 cents offered me off their tendered price. No wonder he was a billionaire.

While more sophisticated than in poor countries, it is common knowledge that in some places what is perceived as corruption is endemic. In Indonesia, the wharfs are a nightmare for clearing. If you do not pay a facilitation fee to someone, you can be kept waiting for weeks to clear your goods. The local argument was that since three weeks is the NORMAL time for clearing, if you want special service, you are just paying for the extra work. The problem of course is that the NORMAL becomes the standard and gets longer since everyone is busy with the special service.

Of course, First World firms have all these anticorruption clauses they have to be aware of and so the usual way out is for them to hire a local agent to handle the illegal payments, which are then billed as something else such as a management fee. Their hands remain clean and someone else does the dirty work.

A major bilateral donor I dealt with insisted that all new contractors view and complete an online Anticorruption module. One question was, "You have just found your local counterpart siphoning money from the project, is this corruption which should involve you?"

The logical expected response would be, "Yes."

In fact, their answer in the machine was "No, since there is now 'National Execution' and so handling that is the government's responsibility."

These issues are very complicated since the unfortunate part of life is that this bribery and corruption is now endemic in some countries and it is almost impossible to do business without paying. It used to be that some local official would seek out someone from a company and propose that they would help them win the bid if they then paid them a commission. When their selected company won, they would get paid. Now the officials go to EVERY bidder with the same story, so they would not even have to influence the bidding process, just collect from anyone who won. If that was not enough, the system now is basically to pay upfront, or you don't get shortlisted.

But the bottom-line is don't get involved and sleep better at night.

5. Phase Five: The Close

(i) Closing any negotiation is the same as making a sale
"Do you want fries with that?"

(ii) This is the hardest part of negotiation
The wooing in its many forms can take any time into a number of years, but the marriage proposal, if it is to come, is still the tricky part.

In the first instance as with closing any negotiation, there is the thought, "Have I done enough?" "If I pop the question now, will I get the response I want, or will there be a rejection?" If there is a rejection, is that a big NO, or a small no, do I keep on even after the rejection or cut my losses and move on?

And then, there is always a little demon in the back of the mind asking, "Did I do the right thing?" That is, could I have got a better deal or is that girl really the one for me? Or the dread of the report writer or the publishing of a book. Do I finish now, or should I add something more? Have I left anything out? The agony increases even after the close as you suddenly remember where things could have been better.

(iii) Some people are afraid to close so keep talking
Everyone would have come across the salesperson who is trying to get you to buy that TV or vacuum cleaner and because you have not said yes, they keep on and on with all the features until you just walk away to escape and buy the item at a store down the road.

Back to our Romeo thinking about proposing to the girl. Has he done enough to impress or convince her, or should he try something else? The problem is that some people take rejection badly and consequently are too afraid to close and pop the question.

(iv) But the close has to come
Irrespective of how the negotiations are going, the time comes when you just have to close and finalize the deal. The traditional good close in a sale

is "Shall I wrap it up now?" It means that in negotiations one can intimate that they have now reached an agreement and so we can settle even when the other side has not actually said yes. Remembering us as herd animals, humans do not naturally like to argue and sometimes if another person makes a decision for us, the person can be grateful rather than having to decide that themselves.

(v) Let the close be on your timing

In a close, of course, either side can initiate the decision. The salesman as said earlier, can say "Shall I wrap that up for you," making the decision for you. However, ideally, the close should be when you want it to be. Timing can be critical since it may be necessary to close if negotiations are heading off in the wrong direction. Alternatively, you might want to keep things going to get more of what you want.

A famous Mr. Len at one development bank would leave people to debate all day before summarizing what he had already prepared in his Memorandum of Understanding. This would be presented for signature just before everyone knew they had to head for the airport and their flights back home.

Remember there is always another flight.

(vi) Are you really closed?

As mentioned in the Introduction, in the famous 1981 book *Getting to Yes* by Roger Fisher and William Ury, touted as being used at camp David between the Palestinians and Israel, their idea was basically as indicated in the subheading, "Negotiating agreement without giving in," that you just kept talking until the other side said "Yes." And we know how well that went, despite Professor Galbraith saying the book was "By far the best thing I've ever read about negotiation." The book uses "insist" and "demand" in various areas, highlighting this dominance approach of trying to railroad one side's opinion through. William Fry, in 1991 followed this up with his book, *Getting Past NO* with a bit more of the same. Just wear them down. However, remember the old adage, "A man convinced against his will is of the same opinion still."

So, when you have a close, make sure you have it. As a minimum in agreements, one can write and sign a Memorandum of Understanding between two sides. In a sale, you have a sales slip or contract. In a marriage, a marriage license for whatever that is worth. But Close.

Having arrived there, any agreement can always be renegotiated….

(vi) One-sided close

A question would be whether an agreement signed in surrender is a result of a negotiation. When the Japanese unilaterally surrendered at the end of the Second World War, one could conclude that the negotiations were the fighting of the war. The Close, the capitulation. On the other hand, the Japanese were let of lightly in comparison to the Germans in their war reparation requirements, so there were some negotiable aspects even then. Trials of war criminals were concessions as were the excuses of the Japanese emperor who, arguably, as head of the nation, even if not personally orchestrating the fighting, was as responsible for his side as Hitler had been for his.

(vii) Deadlock

No matter how much one tries, there are times when negotiations enter a deadlock and there is no forward movement.

Sometimes, as in legal disputes, it is possible to opt for mediation. In some cases, one can call on a lawyer or an expert to clarify or work on some sticking point. The main idea is to keep moving along.

A further option in stalemate is to call for a postponement when it might help people to calm down.

The final option is then always to walk away. This leads into "intransience."

Intransience

In reality, with negotiation, there are times when a persistent situation occurs and no matter what one would like to do or say, nothing will change the other side's opinion. A typical example would be the position and ideology of say Hamas who simply want an end to Israel, which is unlikely to happen, and where from the point of view of both sides there is no compromise.

Getting back to the starting arguments in this text, this position is linked to and through religion, although more one of occupation. But if over 50 percent of the worlds' population follows two main religions that have people believing in myths, how are you going to get any of these to change their mind?

(i) Identifying a persistent position

Historic precedent shows us global persistent situations. Most are a product of religious beliefs. However, major religions were formulated at times when it was believed the earth was flat. Argue against this and you can hit a stonewall.

It is generally accepted that there are 12 major religions in the world, with Hinduism around from some 5,000 to 10,000 BC. Added to these from before Jesus we have Zoroastrianism (3,500 BC), Shintoism (500 BC), Confucianism (551 BC), Jainism 9th century BC, Buddhism in 6th century BC, and Judaism (6th century BC). Those religions formed after Jesus are, of course, Christianity, Islam in 7th century, Sikhism in 15th century, Taoism 126 AD, and Baha'i in 19th century.

The relevance of these rough figures on emergence and acceptance of religious doctrine is their relationship to scientific knowledge of the time they were formed. In this, although it is generally believed Pythagoras in the 6th century BC already believed the earth was not flat, historically, even in Queen Isabella's time Columbus had to sail to America to show the earth was round.

When one looks at these major world religions, one sees that they were almost all formed at a time when scientific general knowledge was not all that great and the people who established the infallible laws by which society had to live might not have had all the answers. Even had they known the earth was round, they expounded that some religious deity had shared the secrets of the universe with them but obviously forgot about the shape of the earth, that refrigeration would come along and earthly societies would later integrate and have to live with each other.

Most of this explains why there has not been an emergence of any major religions in the years since Jesus, just more versions of the same. It would be too difficult to get people to accept the emergence of angels and devils in the light of scientific knowledge. Obviously, there will always be cults of some form to meet founder's agendas and a few have announced they have had Divine intervention, often inspired by drugs. Handy if you want plural wives or to keep women down.

So, if people do not want to accept beliefs of new religions, which would not pass the scientific test, why would they accept dogma laid down at times when people believed the earth was flat when anyone watching a ship sail over the horizon would understand curvature? And why would they fight wars over "My faction of the religion is better than yours, or my God is better than your God?"

Presumably, people need to have something to give them comfort against fear of dying. With a second reason that, as group animals, humanity needs the comfort of sticking to generally accepted theory whether right or wrong. How this will play out in the long run as humanity explores the planets and establishes outposts, for example, on Mars? Only time will tell. The question remains over how long it will take people to reject infallible ideas laid down by people who thought the earth was flat.

Hence, back to the question of how do you relate to and integrate with someone who believes in a philosophy that was formulated when they got this wrong. How do you deal with a persistent proposition?

A logical hypothesis is that in Christianity and Islam as two main religions, having existed for so long, you are not going to change those people's thinking as the concepts are too entrenched as is the fear of death and the unknown. The only way this will change longer term is if science can come up with a provable answer to the death and dying conundrum, giving people an alternative. No alternative, no change.

Meanwhile, we are saddled with a Trump who shows his God-fearing Christianity. One must think if he is the free world, does he really believe in the Bible and all its teachings? It doesn't really matter whether he does believe or not but, in reality, no matter what else he does, for now he has to come over as believing, otherwise he would not have his current job. Whether this is morally justifiable or not is beside the point, but it shows why groupthink has to be employed to get to where we want to be. Trump is not going to tell the American people they got it all wrong.

Consequently, on the Palestinian question, arguing continually over the same issue of Israel's existence needs an alternative. First, one needs to have accepted dialogue as Trump has advanced and after that the need to refocus the argument on alternatives. Not easy, but it can be done. Trump does not have to believe in his side as neither does the other. What they do need to do is forget those positions and get the job done. An American embassy in Jerusalem at least gets everyone's attention.

Moving on from religious beliefs to other areas of intransience, the United States and other Western countries believe in their monarchy steeped in tradition or their constitution to hold them together. Their future is directed by men with short spans of deliberating the future. China believes in its Chinese ethnicity, so there is no time limit to their political agenda.

Constitutions can change. We have amendments. Chinese will still be Chinese. In a thousand years, they will also still be Chinese, so the West does not realize what they are dealing with. The basis is in economic power and how much influence a country can have in the world. China sees that it can now dominate under its totalitarian system and starts to flex its muscle against global opinion.

Attending many diplomatic functions in Beijing, the Chinese treated the representatives from black African countries with disdain. The Africans were left to congregate in their own groups and I never saw any Chinese officials move over to talk to them. It was so noticeable that it was embarrassing. But they can get away with it while it is not acceptable in politically correct societies.

Currently, China has defied international law rulings to claim total ownership of the South China Sea and there is rumor of a possible military base in Vanuatu. They have learned as America did before them, and Britain even earlier, that certain things you can do because you can. This is actually the ultimate bargaining position. Apple might say buy this phone or else, but you can always go to Samsung. China can say "Get lost," and who is going to do anything about it except posture. When China marches in to reclaim Taiwan, who is going to oppose them (when most Taiwanese companies already deal with the Mainland)? Hong Kong may have been handed back to the Mainland, but almost everyone there already had a commercial foot in China. After the takeover, 250,000 children claimed Hong Kong ancestry showing that Hong Kong Chinese businessmen had been busy.

On the donor aid profile, China is pouring money into both Africa and the Pacific, where in the latter region it is now the largest donor after Australia. Flights from Bangkok to Nairobi are full of Chinese workers heading to Chinese-funded projects in Africa. Nothing wrong with that if they want to help, even if historians could infer that this is the next round of colonialism. It does however show up the formal aid process where the EU, World, and Asian Development Banks bound down with their library of rules and regulations compete with Chinese who just arrive with a bag full of money. It is easier to deal one on one than with groups competing with each other.

(ii) Need to move the issues away from the subject

Difficult as it seems, when facing an immovable object, one needs to move around it, not face it head on. A problem seen under Islam has been that the Koran indicates that the word of God was as revealed to Mohammed and cannot be questioned in any way. As this is part of the religion and moving away from or denying anything in the religion can get you killed, it's difficult to get anyone, and in particular the religious leaders to challenge anything in the text. No use pointing out that at the time Mohammed was a wartime leader and what was laid down had a confrontational approach quite logical when fighting a war.

Read the Old Testament and you have the Jews basically being told the same about not challenging the word of God, and even today the Roman

Catholics will ex-communicate any dissenters when found convenient. So, moving around the subject one can spell out the appropriate science and that both the Bible and the Koran were written by humans, and as such fallible beings, only recording what they believed they remembered. There is no record of anything either Jesus or Mohamed themselves were supposed to have written. Perhaps the people who years later wrote the stories got it wrong, since with time as science has come to show us, interpretations can change in light of new knowledge.

Dealing with the Chinese version of persistent, it needs to be explained that once one becomes the master, it is beholding on them to treat their servants well. On the basis that we all have to live on the same planet, it's no use being the master race if everyone else is to be a slave. Slaves don't have money or buying power, so you need a market.

(iii) Catch 22

As Joseph Heller demonstrated in his 1961 novel, *Catch 22*, sometimes you can get into a "double bind." In his story focused on bombardier Captain John Yossarian during the Second World War, where no one really wanted to fly missions, you could get out of flying if you were mad. The problem was that if you admitted you didn't want to fly, that was considered sane since no one wanted to fly, and hence you could not be excused from flying. While the narrative in the novel goes all over the place on the basic stupidity of war, and there appears to be no answer to Catch 22, Milo Minderbinder, the quartermaster with a finger in everything, might accidently have found the answer. He decided it was more convenient for each side to bomb their own side as it saved a lot of flying time, fuel, and casualties, and meanwhile everyone could make a profit. In effect, Milo's solution to this apparent insoluble logical problem was by moving sideways. It didn't solve Catch 22 but instead removed the need for it if bombing your own meant they wouldn't be shooting at you.

Similarly, with double binds, one can move in parallel to achieve the same ends.

On one assignment in China, the team leader and I had some past history because I believed he was incompetent and was just in the job because he was related to the director. He was doing such a miserable job, I just ignored him, basically had to do his work in a parallel universe until suddenly the powers that be decided who was best at the job and I was moved in as an official replacement team leader.

(iv) Divorce

Leading up to a divorce is one of those persistent situations. First, one must remember that many agreements need to be adjusted over time, and marriage could be considered one of them.

In the fact finding of the negotiation before moving into the committed to a divorce phase, in carrying out due diligence, it might be an idea to consider the following points:

(a) When you think of a place and something you did with your spouse (and or partner), if they are no longer with you, will you have anyone there to make it real, that it ever happened? "If the tree falls in the forest and there is no one there...."

(b) Will you be far worse off financially after the divorce and be able to do all the things you liked doing before?

(c) Is there any chance that a new love might end up the same as your current one, or even worse, now they know you are prepared to divorce if you find someone else?

(d) And in the case of children, what is the real cost to them, not just in what you might have invested in them but how they will feel?

(e) Is there going to be some ethnic or religious retribution that will affect your future new life?

(f) Are all your friends going to abandon you and side with the ex?

Should there be any doubts on any of these issues it might be time to think again. If you still wish to go ahead, back to negotiation mode.

(v) Use a parallel universe

An overreaching concept in negotiation on persistent positions is to leave the door open and work on the peripherals. On these issues, the difficulty is that both sides of the arguments are valid. For example, the Palestinians could well say they had been screwed mainly by the Brits who wanted to solve a Jewish problem to appease their conscience post World War II and allowed the creation of Israel. It's hard to argue with that while, at the same time, saying that the Jews were around before anyway does not help. On the other side, for organizations such as Hamas and the like, saying they will never concede until all Jews are driven out of the area, they must know this will never succeed. Creating mayhem and killing often innocent people on any side is not going to change that, so why continue? What all of this suggests is that, at the end of the day, logic backed by a scientific base must win so there is a need to keep on hammering that thought, so one day it gets through.

Remember the international medium for getting on with anyone is **RESPECT.** No matter whether you agree with someone else's opinions or their beliefs, show respect for the individual and it goes a long way. Gaining that respect also requires showing that you understand their position and the constraints. But, first, you must initiate dialogue.

In Cairo, one time I was trying to establish a university research program and was entertained by the lead professor at the Ago Khan's rooftop extravaganza. During the conversation, my host was pointing out how under his religion everyone had to give a tithe of 2.5 percent, which would go to help the poor. I said I had missed that page and amount as I'd never seen a percentage referred to in the Koran. For some reason the debate involved other academics at other tables and I could see that the general consensus was, "what would I know?" The next day at the university I was met by a delegation of three professors along with my host who apologized and said that I was right as it did say "one-fortieth part" not a percentage, but since this worked out at 2.5 percent, we were both right. The end result led to RESPECT for me since I had shown understanding of where they were coming from and I had no more negotiation difficulties. It demonstrated how two sides can be arguing about the same identical issue but from different perspectives. Luckily, I had spent so many nights in Pakistani hotels where they had the Koran on the bedside tables.

In another negotiation in Egypt, my counterpart became my very good friend. He said that as a good Muslim he did not drink but, in my company, where I did drink, he felt that under the direction that one should make your friends feel comfortable, he would have to drink with me. I seemed to suddenly have a preference for brandy. In other words, even religion can find justifications if they are looked for.

In the Chinese situation, respect also still goes a long way. If one can demonstrate that you have tried to understand and exemplify their position, this will be appreciated. Just remember how Chinese have been treated—mocked and vilified in the past—and see how you would feel.

How many Hollywood movies on Chinese themes had no Chinese actors, but had Caucasian actors pretending? The sign in Bruce Lee's *Enter the Dragon*, saying "No dogs or Chinese allowed."

Live to Fight Another Day

If you have ever survived a plane crash, you would understand the saying, "Any landing you can walk away from is a good one." The same applies to negotiations as these are basically time sensitive.

Recently we have seen where Trump, frustrated by failing to get his removal of Obamacare, seemingly gave up while planning in the background and plotting his retaliation to get what he more or less wanted in a second attempt. Part of the plotting was playing the man, but then that is all part of his negotiation technique.

The point is that even if a negotiation fails one time and there will be disappointment, it might have worked for Napoleon burning the bridges behind him but he still finished on the island of Elba anyway. The palindromic, read backward, "Able was I ere I saw Elba," so it finished up the same way. Don't give up and walk back.

Why Some Countries Are More Successful

In Sterling Seagrave's brilliant 1995 book, *"Lords of the Rim,"* he explains how over the centuries disaffected and exiled Chinese moved from their mainland to populate the countries around the Asian rim, bringing with them their skills and financing expertise. Until recently in Africa, where you had a proliferation of Chinese small businesses you did not have Indians. It appears that one society keeps the high ground and the other goes elsewhere. In the Pacific and on the islands, it can still be seen that in some cases the Indians dominate, while in others the Chinese have stamped their mark.

Looking at why German companies are so successful, part has been not only attributed to their close association with Unions who do not hamper work, but it was also postulated through a 2012 study by the SME Research Institute in Bonn, that since 4,400 major family-owned companies were responsible for 43 percent of all German exports, success was through close family ownership.[1] Alternatively, it could be suggested that it is the German's close-knit followers of Lutheranism[2] with strict work ethic. This is similar to the early Pilgrim settlers in America bound together by their religious faith and the feeling of persecution. Again, there is a religious platform and ostracism governing behavior.

Historically, the Jews were the clever merchants envied for their skill. The reality of course is how one handles the money. In the Jewish case, because so many other occupations were denied them, they developed the financial expertise which was all that was left them. Usury was frowned upon by Christians and Muslims alike so someone had to do it. The Chinese of the Rim, as with the Jews, felt themselves as displaced or

---

[1] Allen, F.E. August 14, 2012. *Forbes Staff.*
[2] Friar Martin Luther (1483–1546) Stamp on Separate Protestant Christian Religion.

disadvantaged, and reacting in their defense established a simple yet complex way of lending money throughout the globe. You established credit in one way or the other and then just had to present a paper with another of the tribe to collect the cash somewhere else in the world. Somehow it all balanced out in the end. The process, as were the people in the pipeline, were kept secret so that no one could copy the system. The essential factor is that you need to have extreme confidence of your group and be able to stick together. The Han Chinese had their ancestral villages and their ethnic origins. The Jews had their religion and the status of global pariahs.

Look around every major city in the world and the biggest buildings are the banks and insurance companies. That's where the money is; so to fully understand negotiation, one needs to understand the handling of money and the systems around its ownership and protection.

In reality, there is personal ownership of money and/or the control of money. What this means is that an individual does not have to legally own wealth but can legally control the wealth with the same benefit. The wealthiest people do not necessarily own very much in their own right but have control over the money via other entities, which usually has major tax benefits. Back again to the people who have felt ostracized over the years such as the Jews who for self-protection devised ways to control such funds. Governments want to tax an individual's wealth and individuals want to give them as little as possible.

There are many ways to control money without actual ownership but that is beyond the text here. In its simplest form, say a father gives his son power of attorney over a Swiss Bank account. The son can operate on that account but he does not own it so can't be taxed on it. In turn, he gives his children their powers of attorney on that account and this goes on. All one needs to know is how to negotiate and where to put the money.

Practice Exercises

When student lawyers are training, they sometimes hold moot (subject to debate) courts where they argue imaginary cases for practice. They either dig up old cases and retry them before a pretend jury or invent their own. This is sometimes also done by law firms with high-profile pending cases to test the material and prevent a blindside. Some people are nominated to play the roles of both sides.

Negotiation techniques can be perfected by practice in most instances. It is one thing to think about what you might do and another having to get up there and follow-through in real life.

The following practice exercises are intended to offer a starting point for individuals and groups to introduce themselves into real-life "moot" practice, which can be developed through life.

With practice exercises, select a topic. See how many participants are required in the *Scenario*. Have someone, not role-playing, write out on a card or sheet of paper what each character is to achieve in the exercise. Give each of the participants one of the sets of instructions. Let them have say five minutes to plan their strategy and then *Negotiate*.

If desirable, set a time limit.

In the role-play, anything goes. Use imagination and try to employ the techniques outlined here.

At the conclusion of the exercise on a time limit or when there is a CLOSE, or if the negotiation is abandoned for lack of result, everyone sits down and goes through the *Debrief*. At this stage, each participant reads out what their objective was supposed to be and how they went about trying to achieve their goals; what negotiation techniques they used. They can also outline where they thought the other players were coming from and where things could have been improved.

There can also be a recap on the techniques used by each person or were perceived to have employed during the negotiation, whether emotion had been utilized or were there any red herrings or dirty tricks.

Experience shows that people really get into this role-playing and it becomes not only a training exercise but also a lot of fun. The lessons learned can remain with us for years to come. *I still remember my first....*

1. Buying a car

Scenario: Husband, Wife, and Mother in law.

The Husband: wants to buy a new car because the old one keeps breaking down. He thinks his wife wants renovations to the house they have been discussing. He wants to get his wife to agree to the car without making her mad since there is a limit to the cash they have.

The Wife: does not want the new car since the breaking down limits his mother's visits. She does not however want to say this. She also does not want the house extensions and have her mother-in-law come to live but can't really say so.

The Mother-in-law: wants the new car because she wants her son at beck and call.

Negotiate:
Debrief:

2. Buying a house

Scenario: The owner, the agent, the purchaser's husband, the purchaser's wife.'

The Owner: The Agent said to leave negotiations to him, but the owner still wants $1.3 million although the agent said it should be $1.1 million tops. The Owner wants the best price but realizes he might have to drop expectations.

The Agent: wants to get as much as possible but is caught by telling the Owner $1.1m while believing, in reality, it is only worth $900,000.

The purchaser husband: Does not like the house or want to buy it even when his wife wants it, so he will argue they can't go above $900,000, hoping that will kill the deal.

The purchaser wife: The wife really likes the house as it is just what she wanted, and would go to $1.3m even if she knows the husband does not want to be burdened by a mortgage. She believes that she always gets what she wants in the end.

Negotiate:
Debrief:

3. Talking a police officer from giving you a speeding ticket

Scenario: The Driver, The Driver's wife, The Police officer, The Driver's Mother-in-Law

The Driver: Has to talk the police around to get out of a ticket since there no more points left on his license.

The Driver's wife: Wants the husband booked as he speeds all the time. If he loses his license, then she will be able to take the car to work.

The Police officer: Would be prepared to let the driver off since the speed was not excessive but at least wants to teach the driver a lesson.

The Driver's Mother-in-law: Wants son-in-law to keep license so he can collect her on weekends and hates her daughter's driving.

Negotiate:
Debrief:

4. Facing an interview panel for a job

Scenario: The Applicant, the Chairman of Committee, Committee 1, Committee 2, Committee 3.

The Applicant: Knows this is an important job with the Ministry of Trade and although qualified through past experience he has not previously had employment in the government.

The Chairman: Is fair and prepared to give the applicant a good hearing.

Committee 1: Knows the applicant has no previous government experience so would like to show the applicant up as not having applicable qualifications.

Committee 2: Has come from the private sector and will support the applicant.

Committee 3: Just wants to finish quickly and go to lunch.

Negotiate:

Debrief:

5. Office situation

Scenario: The Secretary, The Boss, The Office Manager, and other female employee.

The Secretary: Wants a new computer.

The Boss: Does not want to spend the money on a new computer.

The Office manager: Wants new computers when he can get them.

The Other Female Employee: Does not want the secretary to have a better computer than hers and is secretly seeing the Boss.

Negotiate:

Debrief:

6. Negotiating a raise

Scenario: The Employee, the Boss, and the Union Representative.

The Employee: He has been at the company for five years without a raise and wants at least a 10 percent increase or will look for another job. To negotiate, the employee asks for 20 percent. He is good at work so needn't worry about finding a new position, but partner is sick and it would be better not have to change jobs right now.

The Boss: The boss does not want to give a raise because turnover is still sluggish but can't afford to lose the employee. He does not want any across-the-board salary increase for all employees. He thinks the extra could be made up with overtime allowances or extra leave.

The Union Representative: Union elections are coming up, so he wants to ensure that members see a push on wages. Hence, he wants the employee to get a big raise, and he will use anything to achieve this.

Negotiate:

Debrief:

7. Dealing with government

Scenario: The Government clerk, the Householder opposite, the neighbor most effected, McDonalds representative wanting to open a store opposite your house.

The Clerk: The clerk has been called in to adjudicate on the objections of two neighbors against the proposed new store. His Boss who does not like him said to fix it "Or else."

The householder: The householder does not want McDonalds to build there for good reason as he is getting on in age and does not want to move.

The neighbor: The neighbor does not want McDonalds but sees this as an opportunity to get some compensation from McDonalds who might even buy his house at an inflated price.

McDonalds: The rep sees this as a prime location for future growth and has been told to see what he can do without stirring up the locals.

Negotiate:

Debrief:

8. Investment proposals

Scenario: The Bank Manager, the investor, the investor's financial adviser

The Bank Manager: The bank manager comes from a conservative branch office where they had to be sure there is no chance of a bad debt.

The Investor: The investor wants to open a restaurant in a good location within a shopping mall. He has run similar restaurants in the past with limited success although a qualified chef.

The Investor's Financial Adviser: The financial adviser does not really want to be there and just wants to do his thing, be able to bill his fee and get out of there.

Negotiate:

Debrief:

9. Negotiating a development contract

Scenario: The successful Bidder, the Donor Agency, The Client.

The Bidder: The bidder won the contract to deliver services to the government of *Uzbanda* and wants to get the full proposed contract price for the five-year assignment.

The Donor Agency: The Donor Agency wants to finalize the contract but at 20 percent below what had initially been proposed.

The Client: The Client is the government of *Uzbanda* who wants the work done but wants to select its own nationals and not those proposed by the Bidder for political reasons. They want to select the nationals, so they can control them and have them pay a fee for selection.

Negotiate:

Debrief:

10. Negotiating a fuel contract

Scenario: The Fuel company rep, The Company representative, the company Managing Director

Fuel company rep: The fuel company rep knows that the company has 280 fleet vehicles so wants to supply petrol to their company pumps and has secretly offered the company representative with whom he is dealing a 5c a liter kickback.

Company rep: The company rep is incensed at having been offered a bribe. The rep has reported this to the managing director and recommended that the bid be rejected and that the company should chose the next lowest bid.

Managing Director: The managing director just wants to have the lowest price for fuel no matter the arrangements.

Negotiate:

Debrief:

11. Buying selling a commercial computer system

This is a commercial situation with multiple players including government.

Scenario: Salesman 1, Salesman 2, Sales Manager, Russian Buyer 1, Russian Buyer 2, Trade Department Representative, Government Security operative.

Salesman 1: Salesman 1 has two levels of supercomputer to sell, one at $3.5 million and the other at $2.3m. He wants to get his sales score up and try to get the top amount.

Salesman 2: Salesman 2 does not like Salesman 1 so will try and sabotage the sale in any way possible without it being too obvious.

Sales Manager: The sales manager is not worried which computer system is sold as long as a sale is made.

Russian Buyer 1: The Russian Buyer 1 desperately wants the top system since Russia does not have similar technology and the government wants to get one to deconstruct and copy.

Russian Buyer 2: Russian Buyer 2 just wants to buy a system and is not involved with Russian government.

Trade Department Representative: The trade department representative wants the sale since this would be good for government policy and should start an ongoing industry selling into Russia.

Government Security Operative: The government security operative is prepared to have the lower-capacity computer sold but not the top one for security reasons. If the sale of the top one looks like going ahead, the government will need to step in to block the sale.

Negotiate:

Debrief:

Important Note: **In negotiation, remember never to tell a lie as it will come back to bite you. There are however many ways of telling the truth...**

Make Up Similar Scenarios Hinged to Own Line of Work or Personal Experience

Research, Research, Research…

Do your due diligence, the other side's strengths and weaknesses in a SWOT analysis just as you do your own. Organizations have agendas as do individuals.

About the Author

Peter Nelson is an Australian economist and accountant who runs his own global chartered accounting firm and consulting company. He has worked commercially and for all major donors in 52 countries, having also run the EU's largest project across China. His specialty has been on economic restructuring and delivery of negotiating seminars, now attempting to look to the future and what that might bring. In his spare time, he is an avid scuba diver and has raced his yacht internationally.

Seminars available from P J Nelson & Co. Pty Ltd
www.pjnelsonco.com pjnelsoncopl@gmail.com
Peter Nelson dr_peter_nelson@yahoo.com

Index

OTHER TITLES FROM THE ECONOMICS AND PUBLIC POLICY COLLECTION

Philip Romero, The University of Oregon and
Jeffrey Edwards, North Carolina A&T State University, Editors

- *How the Information Revolution Remade Business and the Economy: A Roadmap for Progress of the Semiconductor Industry* by Apek Mulay
- *Money and Banking: An Intermediate Market-Based Approach, Second Edition* by William D. Gerdes
- *Basic Cost Benefit Analysis for Assessing Local Public Projects, Second Edition* by Barry P. Keating and Maryann O. Keating
- *International Economics, Second Edition: Understanding the Forces of Globalization for Managers* by Paul Torelli
- *The Commonwealth of Independent States Economies: Perspectives and Challenges* by Marcus Goncalves and Erika Cornelius Smith
- *Econometrics for Daily Lives, Volume I* by Tam Bang Vu
- *Econometrics for Daily Lives, Volume II* by Tam Bang Vu
- *The Basics of Foreign Exchange Markets: A Monetary Systems Approach, Second Edition* by William D. Gerdes
- *Universal Basic Income and the Threat to Democracy as We Know It* by Peter Nelson

Announcing the Business Expert Press Digital Library

Concise e-books business students need for classroom and research

This book can also be purchased in an e-book collection by your library as

- a one-time purchase,
- that is owned forever,
- allows for simultaneous readers,
- has no restrictions on printing, and
- can be downloaded as PDFs from within the library community.

Our digital library collections are a great solution to beat the rising cost of textbooks. E-books can be loaded into their course management systems or onto students' e-book readers.
The **Business Expert Press** digital libraries are very affordable, with no obligation to buy in future years. For more information, please visit **www.businessexpertpress.com/librarians**. To set up a trial in the United States, please email **sales@businessexpertpress.com**.

www.ingramcontent.com/pod-product-compliance
Lightning Source LLC
Chambersburg PA
CBHW071159200326
41519CB00018B/5290